Never be afraid to tread the path alone.
Know which is your path and follow it wherever it may lead you;
do not feel you have to follow in someone else's footsteps.

—Eileen Caddy

Tradition becomes our security, and when the mind
is secure it is in decay.

—Jiddu Krishnamurti

Live life to the fullest. You have to color outside the lines
once in a while if you want to make your life a masterpiece.
Laugh some every day. Keep growing, keep dreaming,
keep following your heart. The important thing is
not to stop questioning.

—Albert Einstein

Scribbles
in the Margins

Discovering Genesis AGAIN for the First Time

MARLIN BROWN

THE NET BIBLE®, New English Translation (NET) Scripture and/or notes
quoted by permission. Quotations designated (NET) are from the NET Bible®
copyright ©1996–2016 by Biblical Studies Press, L.L.C. All rights reserved.

Scripture quotations marked RSV are from the Revised Standard
Version of the Bible, copyright © 1946, 1952, and 1971 National
Council of the Churches of Christ in the United States of America.
Used by permission. All rights reserved worldwide.

Added emphasis in Scripture quotations throughout is denoted by italics.

Cover and book interior design: Rosemary Strohm

ISBN: 978-1-966840-78-7 (paperback)
ISBN: 978-1-966840-79-4 (hardcover)
ISBN: 978-1-966840-77-0 (ebook)

For
Arnold Brown,
Jack Mottweiler,
&
"Uncle" Paul Kugler

My father, my pastor, and my dad's best friend.
You three took the time to stop and listen to this kid.
For that, I am grateful.

CONTENTS

Primal Beginnings

Brothers at Arms

Thoughts About God

Other (Mostly) Genesis Thoughts

Acknowledgments

Tyler and Kelsey, my beloved children, you are who this book is for. You hold in your hands the summation of all those years of my rants about the Bible, religion, and the church. I am able now, finally, to say what the stories were truly about—and why that matters. I remember your eye rolls and sighs. I'm sorry. Still, you put up with me, and for that, I thank you.

John and Cindy, your friendship and interest have been a bastion of loyalty as this work came together. I have ever admired you both. To see and hear you two ask and offer encouragement kept me writing—first, so as not to disappoint, but as the words came easier, it became an eagerness to inform others about what matters to me.

I wish also to acknowledge Landmark Worldwide. Everyone there, paid staff and volunteers, saw me and my work as being of worth. The energy and commitment in seeing me as my possibility fulfilled. Such outlook and belief strengthen my mind and empowers my future.

Most important to this work is my best friend, Lou Ann. You are present for the *aha*! moments, sharing in my delight as well as being present when the silliness of tradition overwhelmed me. I remember you doing a happy dance as I unlocked some hidden gem with me a few times! You were also supportive of my pain when I railed against the time lost from my life before learning these truths—those gems of understanding that were never taught, neither from the pulpit nor in Sunday school. At times, your genuine questions were annoying, but during those inquisitions, ideas and possibilities sprang forth. I found clarity in your responses. More importantly, far too often, you pointed out the alien on my face that kept me from seeing what was there in plain sight.

Mere words are not enough—but thank you all.

Author's Statement of Belief

How I Know There Is a Cosmic Creator God

I see the sunrises over the Catalina mountains in Southern Arizona. They are different every day, yet they are immortal. I wonder at the delicate flowers of a defiant cholla cactus. I marvel at the muted, soft power of a snowfall. That's how I know.

Also hearing the laughter of children playing. Smiling when I hear the crack of a bat on a spring day. Attending a sporting event and knowing there will be fifty-six thousand friends there I have never met before. Smelling a pine forest. Hearing the trees whispering as the wind blows through and the birds chirping as they do their birdy things.

Standing on the shore of Lake Superior during a late November storm, feeling its power and chaos. Seeing the effects of the wind as it blows across a field of wheat—the waves and troughs as the wind undulates on its way from here to there.

Seeing photos from the James Webb telescope situated a million miles from mother earth, showing black holes, other galaxies, and stars older than time itself. Learning of the tiniest components that make up every atom of my being. Discovering there are rules that make those tiniest of tiny things work together—and, within those rules, the allowance for me to sit here and write.

Understanding that even though the blue marble I call home is billions of years old, there is structure and logic to how it works and how its inhabitants fit so neatly into the entire scheme of life. All of these things prove the existence of a Cosmic Creator God to me.

Philosophy of God

I do not believe in god.

That statement has a loophole, you see; that loophole allows me the choice to accept or not accept that there is a god. My god is as real to me as the chair I sit in. I do not consider if, when I sit, this chair will hold me. The concept of *chair* is so foundational that there is no possibility for a choice about it. The same is to be said about breathing. I do not consider if the next breath I take will happen, for it is intrinsic to my being that breathing *is*.

That is my concept of my god. No belief is necessary.

My god is so foundational to me that through the travels I have endured while creating this book, there has been one unassailable constant. There is a god—one who is the cause and causation of what is written in the anthology called the Bible. What that god wants is to be in communion with me, and me with him. Nothing more, nothing less.

I have no reason to argue pro or con regarding this idea, nor to argue the reality of a word such as *justice*. I cannot touch, feel, smell, or taste justice, but justice *is*. Just as god, Adonai, or even YHWH is.

There must be something real to have allowed this god, the god of Abraham, Isaac, and Jacob, to have lasted over two millennia. Not only lasted but grown and developed. I do not mean the religions that are in his name, but the foundational thought process. And respect and homage must be paid to that dynamic.

Philosophy of Religion

I am not a fan of religion. That is from the baggage of my childhood. Religion is good in that it helps to define basic outlines of belief. Where it goes wrong is when any set of people demand the agreement of others to believe as they see fit—as if religion were a club. Jesus of Nazareth did not demand conformity for any religious structure, but to focus wholly on what was important. What was important to him was the recognition of what god wanted from his creation—conversation. All else is commentary.

Final Note

To my readers—This is who I am, and this is my declaration. I am unashamed.

To my father—Dad, I finally know what I believe.

Introduction

Forests of trees and oceans of ink have been spilled writing works that purport to explain the intricacies of what is inside the two Judeo-Christian testaments known as the Bible. The authors of these treatises—in most cases[1] and with a deep and abiding respect for their faith—worked to further an understanding of what was between the covers of that book. Their works strive to answer questions that have been around for several thousands of years, and I applaud them in their endeavors.

We of today consider the writings inside the Bible from our perspective and declare they are germane to our lot at this time. This is unfortunate, for the authors did not know their words would be around in our time. Their world is not ours, nor must we insist that it be so. An example of this concept is found in the Christian idea of how the Hebrew testament, the *Tanakh*, shows a distinct line of progression toward Jesus of Nazareth's ministry. How can that be?

Original sin and the Trinity, concepts not mentioned in the Tanakh, are found inside its words by Christian writers who want to add weight and credence to the theological stance offered by St. Paul. The mighty and delicious works of the Tanakh's authors are even relegated into the "old and busted" dustbin by Christians, easily proved by their nomenclature of that work—the "Old" Testament. Yet, inside these "old" writings are found the essence of what Jesus of Nazareth preached and taught to his followers.

---

1   Yes, I am looking at you, Bultmann.

Upon reading Deuteronomy and Jeremiah, one will see that the words of Jesus (not St. Paul) ring with clarity and force.

All things evolve from their original inception.[2] History as we know it depends on the facts of what happened. That's today's world. In ages past, this was not so. Timelines were not important, nor were the fussy details of who, what, when, and how. Time and space often got expanded or contracted to fit the important idea—that of making things fit the storyline for the desired outcome. In the *Sitz im Leben*[3] of the Hebrew texts, this is the driving force. Oral tradition, until the advent of the printing press, was the way teachings were presented. As we see in the Gospel accounts of Jesus, metaphorical stories carried the day.[4]

The origin of metaphorical stories comes from the ancient and hoary past. Through what we know as myth, we see our ancestors in their attempts to understand the reality of the world as they knew it. No, these myths were not lies, nor stupid stories. They were real, and we, if we are honest, are to be inspired by the beautiful understanding of how those myths described their world. Myth evolved into a metaphor, which is still used today to describe truths in simple, everyday language. The Old Testament is filled with metaphor, even with myth, especially in the first book of Genesis. The first eleven chapters are filled with origin stories of how and why life is the way it appears. No one of that age accepted those stories to be a literal rendering of history, yet they saw the underlying truth, which was the most important detail of the stories.

As life went on, through the oldest cultures, these stories were accepted—since what they described was as good as truth. The import behind the stories faded into the background as the stories themselves began to be viewed and presented as the truth. That is, until four men threw a monkey wrench into that long-held set of traditions. One man pointed a telescope into the night sky. Another created moveable type and the printing press.

---

2   With the exception of horseshoe crabs, sharks, and evangelical fundamentalist thinking.

3   *Sitz im Leben*: Setting in life—a term coined by Hermann Gunkel to denote why a text was created as well as its purpose and function at that time.

4   These metaphorical stories by Jesus are known as parables. Simply put, a parable is a story that illustrates a moral or religious lesson.

Another, a humble catholic priest, translated the Bible into the common tongue. The last was an irritable but brilliant scholar of Jewish birth who was kicked out of both the Jewish and Catholic churches for insisting the religions were not asking the right questions of the Bible.[5]

We are still seeing the tremors and tidal waves of the actions of those men. The printing press gave general literacy a necessary push. The ability to read the Bible in one's own language gave humanity a personal understanding of its powerful words. Critical study of both reality (science) and traditional theology provides the chance to strip away tradition, which obscured all of the truths lying beneath. Yet there are those today who have created great theological and philosophical walls against the hidden (in plain sight, if only we looked!) insights into the Bible's pages.

Inside the pages of this treatise, one will find the author's intent to glean the gold found by a simple reading and consideration of the setting of the Bible during the life of the author. This requires research into other cultures from the time of the writing and before, including religions, architecture, societal norms, languages, and excavated writings from those civilizations.

My father would chide me whenever I attempted to explain something using the word being explained. This is known as circular reasoning and is to be ignored when presented. Much of the evangelical and fundamentalist reasoning of the last century is based upon this idea, which we will discuss further in the following chapters.

What I present is not theology, nor is theology wanted, although there will be some metaphysical mumbo-jumbo occasionally. Too much theology, especially in the last one hundred fifty years, is a recirculation of ideas. A wash-rinse-repeat cycle, if you will. These concepts are earworms today, sticky, trite theology that pervades one's mind until there is no real semblance of meaning. Of course, in today's churches, Joe and Jane Pewsitter are not challenged in any way, shape, manner, or form to take any action on a personal level toward gaining their own understanding.

The ideas presented here are selective and not comprehensive. Many times,

---

5   Galileo Galilei, Johannes Gutenberg, Martin Luther, and Baruch Spinoza, respectively.

only a part of a story is offered when compared to the overall storyline. This is intentional, for inside these tidbits are where the theology, philosophy, and tradition do not fit what is written. Here is where the questions asked and the answers offered imply that we are looking incorrectly. Instead, you will read how considering another way of thinking (asking a different question) allows the truth of the story to shine forth, just as it did when the Bible was written.

Along the way, other truths will spring forth. Most certainly, those truths will cause issues and consternation to some. For while scholars, theologians, and even seminary students know the truth, Joe and Jane are not told for fear of the upset it might cause. I was shocked but heartened to learn that Moses did not write the Pentateuch and that there were three Isaiahs who, over several hundred years, wrote the beautiful book of that name. A mistranslation made Mary a virgin. Cain did not marry his sister either. Did the flood really happen—and if so, when? We discuss that also, but with the knowledge that it does not really matter, for the truth inside the story cares not. And no, the world was not created in six days.

Archaeology was an anchor for this book. What is found in the ground has led to delightful knowledge unknown to even people in George Washington's day. The Royal Library of Ashurbanipal, excavated in Nineveh, has provided a wealth of knowledge. Ras Shamrah (the ancient city of Ugarit) led to a complete reassessment of ancient Canaan. What has been unearthed in Israel tells a whole different story of what the United Kingdom of David and Solomon looked like. The Armana tablets, found in Egypt, also give valuable insight into the discussion. We must not forget the treasure trove of the Dead Sea Scrolls. Do any of these invaluable finds discount or dismiss what is inside the Old Testament? No, not at all. That question demands the ancients conform to our system of thinking.

Galileo Galilei was the first to stretch our understanding of what tradition offered, but it was not until the seventeenth century when geology forced people to accept that Genesis was built on metaphor, not fact. Imagine this: Isaac Newton did not know of dinosaurs. Nor did he know of the continents and how they moved. He was still processing the size of the world and the new land masses found a mere hundred years before! We now look at the world in a new way, processing with rigor and logic and experimentation. The ancient writers did the same thing, just differently.

All this is to say that this book offers the freedom to think about ancient stories in new and delightful ways. There is no demand for the reader to accept what is found inside. Try the ideas on, see if they fit for you. With the brain god gave this author and the research tools online and on my shelves, I conclude that these ideas work well and do not negate any storyline. Rather, the concepts allow for fresh air that assists the truth inside those metaphors (myths) to be seen again. Take a ride and enjoy!

One last statement: I apologize for nothing between the covers of this book.

CHAPTER 1

The Secret Sauce

*Once upon a time, in a land far, far away,
across a deep, dark ocean, there was ...*

And so began another story by my father. That simple phrase caused kids aged one to ninety-two to sit up, eager eyes and ears focused on my father's next words. His stories were epic—fun and riveting, abounding with twists and unexpected turns. The ending could be a pun, evoking groans and laughs of appreciation. Other times, a very chaste tale could have a rather ribald ending (interesting, coming from a minister). He could easily weave a moral or philosophical insight that left his hearers thinking, *Hmmmm.*

My father was a humble man who was raised in the home of poor sharecroppers in the Missouri River Valley of Iowa during the Great Depression. His greatest mentors were those who sought after the simple and profound in life. Being able to discern the obvious in situations where the conversations skewed from one side to the other, his stories could always emphasize the simple truth. Why, you ask, do I bring up my father and his penchant for engaging in discussion via, dare I say, parables? It was his way of expressing simple truth from inside the complications that humans bring to the table. Not only did his stories create a vivid memory but they connected with his audience in a much more profound way. He brought life and delight into conversations that bordered on the arcane and confusing.

For example, when telling of the children of Israel crossing the Jordan River, my father painted such a picture of that momentous event: the mighty rushing river was stopped when the feet of the men who were carrying the Ark of the Covenant touched the roaring waters. Picture yourself as one of those people; can you see the water on the upstream side getting "heapier and heapier, towering higher and higher as you went marching past?" Close your eyes. Put yourself in that moment. Feel the terror—and, yes, the delight of that great working of your god!

In another water-related story, the children of Israel crossed the Sea of Reeds with the pharaoh's wheeled chariots hot on their heels. The sea had just parted, revealing a dry passage, which you and your family were to cross to safety. My father said, "I am sure several young children stuck their fingers in those massive walls of water as they crossed. Just like a kid does on a wall as they walk along," and "Look over there. There is a father making his kids laugh as he pokes at the surprised fish on the other side of that wall of water. Do you think dad stuck his fingers in his ears and waggled them?"

I speak of my father now, for he relates to the topic of this chapter. What was the "special sauce" my father used when creating a story? In the larger context, what is the special sauce that has kept the Bible and its teachings around and alive for millennia? This is the topic we will consider now. Despite my dislike of anything and everything French, the French language has a term that nicely answers the question: *je ne sais quoi* (something that cannot be adequately described or expressed). That something is the spark that enlivens the Tanakh. It is also how the Christian testament, though in a clunky way, fits easily with the Tanakh.

Scholars and preachers over the centuries have worried this question like a dog with a chew toy, never quite clueing into the secret, the ace in the hole, the smoking gun, the "it" factor, the simple, obvious answer from the outset, the truth. The question, I realized, being asked by those honored scholars and philosophers was not properly formatted. One does not "get" the answer, for the question was being asked only inside the Judeo-Christian religious structure. Comparing something to itself, then asking what's the difference, is circular and rather silly. The actual answer is to consider an outside source for comparison. In the last two centuries, that outside source has revealed itself: Judeo-Christian theology needed to compare to the other religions that were extant in its early days of development. I refer to the Hittites in Anatolia and the Canaanites, whose focal point was in Ugarit, to the north of Israel. The Akkadian, Assyrian, Babylonian, and Sumerian cultus was a composite of the Mesopotamian religious system. Egyptian hieroglyphics reveal a vast system of belief structures. Religions like these were far older than the Hebrew newcomer. Their influence and beliefs impacted and influenced the young Hebrew cult, despite the polemics thrown against them. Christianity took form during the heyday of Greek and Roman influence.

Out of this polyphony, through the ages, only one god remained.

The stories and mythologies of these ancient gods are hauntingly familiar when considered. Mesopotamia's creation saga, the *Enuma Elish*, causes one to see another take on the Hebrew creation story. The Sumerian Atra'hasis epic voyage reminds us of Noah and his sea journey. Roman and Greek gods creating humans gives us pause for its familiarity. The Norse god Odin (All-Father) was the leader of souls and predicted the outcome of Ragnarök, the ending of the world—much like that odd book of Christian fame, the book of Revelation.

The greatest common denominator between these past, dead religions is how humankind is looked upon. Humans were an afterthought. Humans were only created to do the scutwork of the gods. Kings and heroes were only the concern of the gods, and even then were only to provide for the pantheon. At death, humans were sent to a place that was the cosmic opposite of the heavens. No, not hell as described by the Christians, which is filled with torment—but somewhere boring and dull. Imagine the waiting room scene at the end of the movie *Beetlejuice*, and you will get the picture.

Before the exile in 586 BCE, the Hebrews phrased the afterlife as "sleeping with my fathers," which was much in line with the other cults. Other religions depict humanity being made from the dust of the earth, mixed with a god's blood. That god who is donating the blood is a god who went against the wishes of the other gods—a corrupt god, in other words. Why has humanity involved itself with that type of blood? That is not hard to understand, for humans are corrupt, but we have a bit of "god" in us. Only if humans contain that spark, however degenerate, can humanity serve the gods properly.

In the Babylonian *Enuma Elish*, Marduk, the high god, creates man like this:

> "I will establish a savage, 'man' shall be his name. Verily, savage man, I will create. He shall be charged with the service of the gods that they might be at ease! The ways of the gods I will artfully alter ... Who was it that contrived the uprising and made Tiamat rebel and joined battle? Let him be handed over who contrived the uprising. His guilt I will make him bear that you may dwell in peace!" ... It was Kingu who contrived the uprising, and made Tiamat rebel, and joined battle. They bound him, holding him before Ea. They imposed on him his guilt and severed his blood (vessels). Out of his blood, they fashioned mankind. He imposed the service and let free the gods.

With the understanding of how humanity fits into the other religions' respective schemes, we turn to the ideals set forth in the Hebrew writings, and eventually the Christian outlook as well. Genesis 1, the first creation story, shows man and woman being created as the final act. There is no using blood or dust in this first chapter, for a simple command suffices. The Cosmic Creator God offers man and woman a special prize, which gives our first clue to humanity's importance to the Hebrew god. Genesis 2 brings the dust idea to the forefront. In this chapter, we see the very first creation act: the god forms man out of the dust of the ground. Handmade (does the Cosmic Creator God have hands?), enlivened with the very breath of that very same god! Man is enlivened with a part of his creator!

> Then God said, "Let us make humankind *in our image, after our likeness.*"
> —Genesis 1:26 (RSV)

> The LORD God formed the man from the soil of the ground and *breathed into his nostrils the breath of life,* and the man became a living being.
> —Genesis 2:7 (RSV)

Now we have something that is wildly different from those other religions. People were a special creation, the *unique* part of creation. We see something special about this act and the result. Genesis 1 speaks of humanity being made in the god's image. No other creation gets that option. Genesis 2 tells of the god's breath being the animator. No other creation gets the breath of the god. Okay, we might be onto something, but so far, we have nothing that elevates the entire storyline of the Bible that has kept the concepts going for so long.

How do the primordial stories work with the patriarchs in Genesis? What is the connection between Exodus and the histories of what has gone before? How do we relate the ribald Song of Solomon and the droll Ecclesiastes to that distinct act? The prophets must also be in accordance somehow with this hidden *je ne sais quoi*. We must not forget Jesus and his stuff, either. What is the key to the longevity in that cycle of writings that has impacted the entire world's population? The answer, my friends, is not blowing in the wind. It sits there (written) in plain sight, looking at us and saying, "Look at me!"

> And God blessed them, and *God said to them*, "Be fruitful and multiply, and fill the earth and subdue it; and have dominion over the fish of the sea and over the birds of the air and over every living thing that moves upon the earth." And *God said*, "Behold, I have given you every plant yielding seed which is upon the face of all the earth, and every tree with seed in its fruit; you shall have them for food. And to every beast of the earth, and to every bird of the air, and to everything that creeps on the earth, everything that has the breath of life, I have given every green plant for food." And it was so. —Genesis 1:28–30 (RSV)

> And the LORD *God commanded* the man, *saying*, "You may freely eat of every tree of the garden; but of the tree of the knowledge of good and evil you shall not eat, for in the day that you eat of it you shall die."
> —Genesis 2:16–17 (NRSV)

> And they heard the sound of the LORD God walking in the garden in the cool of the day, and the man and his wife hid themselves from the presence of the LORD God among the trees of the garden. But the LORD God called to the man, *and said to him*, "Where are you?" *And he (Adam) said*, "I heard the sound of thee in the garden, and I was afraid, because I was naked; and I hid myself." —Genesis 3:8–10 (RSV)

I must admit, I felt rather stupid when the lightbulb turned on. The Cosmic Creator God speaks to man (humankind, if you prefer). Even better, humanity can speak to their god directly, without any intermediary! In other creation accounts, humanity was seen only as a tool the gods used to suit their purposes—not to have a dialogue with, let alone interact as if the humans were important and worth caring about. Kings or sovereigns only joined the godly festivities sometimes.

Immediately, my mind was overwhelmed with other conversations between the Cosmic Creator God and people. Cain's conversations, both before and after his brother Abel's demise. Abraham had talks with his god continually through his life, even (respectfully, I will add) going toe-to-toe and arguing for redemption regarding the impending doom of Sodom and Gomorrah. Moses, well—he was BFFs with the Cosmic Creator God. Moses talks his god down from destroying the children of Israel after they pull some stupid stunts. His god soothes Moses when he is ready to quit the game. Moses gets to meet his god face-to-face, even! Okay, the face-to-face part is not true, but for good reason:

> And Moses said, "Show me your glory." And the LORD said, "I will make all my goodness pass before your face, and I will proclaim the LORD (Yahweh) by name before you; I will be gracious to whom I will be gracious; I will show mercy to whom I will show mercy." But he added, "You cannot see my face, for no one can see me and live." —Exodus 33:18–20 (RSV)

We also witness the Cosmic Creator God having a picnic with Moses and seventy leaders.

> Moses and Aaron, Nadab and Abihu, and the seventy elders of Israel went up, and they saw the God of Israel.[1] Under his feet there was something like a pavement made of sapphire, clear like the sky itself. But he did not lay a hand on the leaders of the Israelites, so they saw God,[2] and they ate and they drank. —Exodus 24:9–11 (RSV)

Exodus 20 tells of Elohim speaking directly to the entire assembly of Israel with the covenant. Upon hearing his voice (vv. 18–20), the people told Moses

---

1   Hebrew: the Elohim.
2   Hebrew: Elohim of Israel.

they would rather have Moses as the intermediary instead of being spoken to directly. (The people are terrified, and deservedly so, when the entire assembly hears their god speaking to them directly.)

King David had a very intimate relationship with his god. The prophets all spoke with the god of Israel, and even had long conversations, although some were more lucid than others. Some prophets were not especially nice in those chats. Job went head-to-head with his god. Even though he conceded the argument to the Cosmic Creator God, he maintained that his side of the argument was still valid. His god was good with that disagreement.

The Christian testament offers a new take, for now we see a personalized form of conversation when Jesus of Nazareth is on the scene. He speaks *for* the God of Israel and speaks *with* the God of Israel. Saint Paul's message says that the Cosmic Creator God, through Jesus, wants to commune with us directly (I still do not understand why there needs to be an intermediary, though). And the list goes on through the ages, down even to our day.

If I have not been clear to this point, I will do so now. The Cosmic Creator God created humanity specifically to be in communion with himself. He offered no other part of creation that option. Everything else created was for one purpose—to allow humanity to be fruitful and multiply. And all humanity has that special sauce—to be in communication with the Cosmic Creator God!

Let us consider what we have found so far. Multiple religions reigned during the formation of the Judeo-Christian belief system. They were much older, some by thousands of years, yet they are not in circulation today. One of the core values those beliefs held in common told of humanity being placed far down the list of importance. Humanity was to be played with or to be used for menial labor to enhance the life of the gods. We see only two examples when one god from the pantheon of the gods sided on humanity's side. The Mesopotamian flood myth is one where the human, Atra'hasis, is aided by the god Enki. The other is the Greek god Prometheus, who steals fire from the gods and gifts it to humanity.

We see the Hebrew god acting in a much different way. Both creation stories tell of the Cosmic Creator God planning and executing an environment to enhance and extend the lives of his most desired creation, humanity. Humanity must be able to sustain life, and sustenance was provided— specifically so the conversations would continue. What follows as we read through the rest of the Bible tells us over and again of that desire. Genesis 1–11 shows the primal world of beginnings, of how life is, and, according to the stories, why life is the way it is. These origin stories were placed so readers had a background for the rest of the story yet to be unfolded. The rest of Genesis tells of the origins of those people who become the Children of Israel, his chosen people. In these biographies, we see the god and the heroes in regular conversation. Those conversations were sometimes good, with blessings overflowing—other times flooded with doom or hardship. These heroes were not all good. In fact, they were far from it. They were all the product of those primal beginnings. All of them were in conversation with their Creator God, and he was with them.

In the next epic cycle, the Exodus, the Cosmic Creator God chooses Moses, and we see the successful escape from Egypt, hijinks included. That nation, with the help of Moses and his god, then makes a contract. That contract states that if the people stay in communion, he will be their god. They get a personal god. For the first time in history, a people get a god who is available to them, a personal god who cares for them (most certainly not a people who have to care for the god). Good stuff! The history books—Joshua, Judges, 1 and 2 Samuel, 1 and 2 Kings, and 1 and 2 Chronicles—put that very commitment of their god to work. Referring to the above contract, there was a simple directive known today as the *Shema*: "Hear, O Israel: G-d is our L-rd, is one."[3] Keep to this key point, and their lives would be fruitful, and they would multiply. Problems occur only when the Creator God's one desire is ignored.

The prophets speak to this point. Fifty-four prophets are named in the Tanakh. Eighteen of those prophets have books for our reading pleasure. Their job was to hold the people of Israel accountable for their actions. When the people ignored their god, his prophets were there. The prophets offered solace if the people turned back to following the god's request. If the people did not, well, the prophets spelled doom. The Writings,[4] the remaining

---

3   Hebrew: "Hear you Israel! Yahweh Elohim is our one Yahweh" (Deuteronomy 6:4).

4   Psalms, Proverbs, Job, Song of Songs, Ruth, Lamentations, Ecclesiastes, Esther, Daniel, Ezra-Nehemiah.

books, are personal responses of the good that comes from being aligned with the Creator God's wish, being as humanity was created to be. I will not use the phrase "in a personal relationship with the god," for that shows a status that creation cannot have with its creator. However, the ability to be in conversation is spelled out, as we have seen above.

According to Christian tradition, Jesus of Nazareth was an extra step toward that more personal connection. I dislike that term, for it has been overused and is trite when explaining what is being offered. Yet there is not a better way to define, despite my efforts. Prior to Jesus doing his thing, the Hebrews saw a clear separation that limited a single person from that immediate connection with their god. The logic goes like this: a creation can be much like its creator, but it will never be on a par with the creator. The Cosmic Creator God is therefore holy. His creations are, by being in his image, profane.[5] Therefore, the Hebrews do not say nor even spell their god's name, for putting such a holy word through profane lips will mar the holiness of their god.

The separation held prior to Jesus' appearance on the scene between humanity and the Cosmic Creator God was dissolved. Jesus of Nazareth became a pathway for each and every person to have a more intimate connection with Jesus' god. This level of fellowship was only presented to the entire nation of Israel before (and even during) Jesus' ministry. Gentiles, those outside the Hebrew lineage, were out of luck until St. Paul got into the act and included them. Not that I have a problem with that! Christian testament writings and early apologists worked hard to quantify and define what this relationship meant and looked like. Early on, the time and effort were spent attempting a catchy phrase like the Hebrews had (the Shema), but the myriads of differing opinions put that ideal aside. The Catholic church got lost in the minutiae and lost track of the single desire of their god. The Christian church got so confused and distracted that even they screwed up the Shema.

The question under consideration throughout has been to discover what is special to the longevity of the Bible. Here, now, we are finally able to put the pieces together. The writings inside the Bible show a god who wanted

---

5   Not the bad kind of profane, but merely *not being holy*, as the god is.

something unique for his special creations, man and woman. That god spent effort to create an environment that allowed his creations to flourish, to be fruitful and multiply. The Cosmic Creator God did everything so the man and woman could be in communion with him. He created them with that ability, and that desire, as seen by Jesus' actions and speech.

The Cosmic Creator God occupies a holy space. Man lives in a profane world. The god transcends the separation, but man cannot. Man is designed to "be with," so his god made woman to fulfill that role in the profane world. Both man and woman become one.

> Two people are better than one, because they can reap more benefit from their labor. For if they fall, one will help his companion up, but pity the person who falls down and has no one to help him up. Furthermore, if two lie down together, they can keep each other warm, but how can one person keep warm by himself? Although an assailant may overpower one person, two can withstand him. Moreover, a three-stranded cord is not quickly broken.
> —Ecclesiastes 4:9–12 (NET)

Here we have a gestalt moment! As stated above, the sum becomes greater than the whole. A man and a woman who are of one accord are far stronger in their resolve than alone. A man or a woman with the resolve of their partner will have a stronger communication, both in the profane world and the holy realm. A man and a woman with their god is the completion of the equation. What a grand design! The Creator God gets a three-for-two deal. Humanity (I meant to use that word here) gets a stronger relationship with their god, and their mate. With this in mind, is it not surprising when "God saw everything that he had made, *and behold, it was very good*" (Genesis 1:31, RSV).

People throughout the ages have related to the simplicity of the words in the Bible. When the permutations and hoops, as religions require, are laid aside, the secret sauce is tasted and found welcoming. The story found inside the covers, while old and dated, is filled with references to those people who lived lives much as we do today. We must remember that these works were not penned for us today, but the truths lying in the words are evergreen, even twenty-five centuries later!

Primal Beginnings

CHAPTER 2

Bigger Than Yours!

In the beginning
God made the sky and the earth.
Yet the earth was invisible and unformed,
and darkness was over the abyss,
and a divine wind was being carried along
over the water.[1]

Where better to start than at the beginning. Our first glimpse of what will eventually be sixty-six books about the relationship between the Hebrew god, Yahweh, and his chosen people starts with a view of the primordial time when the cosmos was at its beginning. This chapter is about Genesis 1, the first creation story in the Hebrew Bible. Countless traditions have embedded themselves in our collective consciousness for thousands of years because of this story, fewer than a thousand words long. These traditions are

---

1   Genesis 1:1–2 (LXX).

assumptions, meanings mined in a certain mental framework or biases that are overlaid onto what is written.

When reading and pondering either testament, do any of us acknowledge those biases and work to see past them? We automatically perceive the Genesis writings from our twenty-first-century societal and religious norms. We also combine what we read to align with what we have been taught to believe, both from religious sermons and the accumulated tradition. It is these deep-seated reflexes that must be attended to before we journey into what is going to be difficult for readers to comprehend as we consider the creation story that will unfold below.

Genesis contains two distinct creation stories: a creation story and an origin story. They are divergent and not the same, despite what tradition demands. Regardless of how one attempts to meld these two stories, the harmonization will fail the sniff test (logic). The first story requires great leaps of logic and implied beliefs. It is so detailed that it verges on being pedantic. The other is simpler and cares not for such minutia as the other. We find our second storyline to be fast paced, starting with fantastic delight and boundless joy but with an ultimate outcome that causes us tears and pain in the end. Here we read of only what interests a common person, the daily life of who and what matters in the long run.

Our first story sees man (and woman) created after the animals that inhabit the land, birds who are home in the air, and fish who teem in the sea. The ultimate creation was humans, after which the Cosmic Creator God rested. We are bound into a strict sequence of events defined as "days" for each of the creations, starting with a yawning, black, cavernous chaos from which order is derived. Step by step, the chaos is divided into separate but equal forms of order that allow for another division to appear, which culminates with the penultimate act, the creation of man and woman.

Interesting markers are woven into this seven-day tapestry of the first creation story—sea monsters, unnamed luminaries, humanity, the Cosmic Creator God resting, and a required naming structure—yet we miss out on the true import of the story. Whole traditions and thoughts about the trivia in this story have pummeled us to the point that we cannot launder them out of our consideration of what is literally there on the pages—what the author wished to tell. To our disadvantage, we are unaware of the significance of the important clues. Other ideas have been amplified out of proportion in each generation to serve each generation's purpose.

The older story, the second story, is a compilation of even older oral bits and pieces. The story cares not for any chaos-to-order typology. Tradition implies the earth is already present but without even rain or plant life to be seen. This is on purpose, but it's never spoken about. That is one thing we, as readers, are expected to understand. In the second narrative, a distinct Creator God constructs a secure environment to show his creative power. First, he starts out by forming man to tend the safe space formed for him. Trees and plant life are next. Animals and birds appeared next, finally ending with man's equal, woman. We learn nothing of the occupants of the heavens or of sea or land. The beginning of everything is not a concern. We note that chaos does not exist within the garden. Of the oceans and their denizens, we get no glimpse. Is there life outside the "garden," or is it still a wasteland? We are told nothing, for it matters not to the story. The author knows we are to understand there is a non-garden part of life.

The location of this garden is mentioned, as it holds significance in the story of the ancient listeners. We of today are ignorant of its import. The deliberate absence of a concept of time in our second story is intentional, as the focus is on relationships rather than chronological sequence. Here is the first conundrum we must face. Our traditions insist these two stories are the same, yet different. We have been trained to ignore the fundamental question, which revolves around radically different distinctions, contradictions, and different genres of writing. Literalists argue against the possibility of a contradiction since it will suggest an inaccuracy in one of these stories, and, naturally, a Scripture book cannot be erroneous. Scripture is flawless according to tradition, evangelicals, and literalists who assert that disbelief results in damnation. According to them, these are not different genres, nor are these conflicting stories. Yet these two stories have radically different outcomes in mind, as we see from the words inside them—even in translation! We are here to consider the first creation saga, found in Genesis 1. Here we are to remain for the duration of this chapter.

To acquire understanding of this story, we must divorce ourselves from two thousand years of tradition. When considering who authored this book, we spring the first trap, for here lies the most insidious and pernicious place where the average person becomes confused. Christians demand we accept that Moses, the greatest prophet in Israel's history, authored Genesis and the other four books of the Torah known as the Pentateuch. We are to accept these were written before Moses' death in the fifteenth century BCE. Piece of cake, is it not? Not so fast, for archaeology, biblical criticism, and even theological schools have put these beliefs to the side. These assumptions may be hard to accept, for they are part of long-held tradition, but they are required thoughts about these issues. This will be hurtful to hear, for we grew up learning in Sunday school—as well as from the pulpit—that Moses did the deed. However, it is incorrect.

What is in plain sight in the words has been glossed over by tradition. We ignore the simple truth, for we are programmed that way. If we take off our tradition-colored glasses, what can we glean from the words in our Bible about the authorship? When studying the Bible rigorously *as literature,* we find four or more writers who did the work of what we consider being the first five books of the Hebrew Bible. None were called Moses. We see obviously distinctive styles of writing, although it is exceedingly difficult to see these differences in our English translations. However, in the original Hebrew and Aramaic, such things are noticeable. Careful study will help determine the time frame in which certain stories (or parts of stories) were written. This allows us to see and understand the Sitz im Leben and gain knowledge of the language that was spoken, which idioms were in use, and which words were in style during that age. We see from a consideration of these points, and others, that the first creation story is much newer than the second creation story.

1. If Moses wrote the Torah, in what language did he write? "Hebrew, of course," I hear you say. Especially the hardliners out there who claim the whole exodus event took place in the mid-fifteenth century BCE. However, Hebrew as a language was not even in its

primal stage. The Hebrew language was finally being separated from the Canaanite language and script in the tenth century BCE. Moses and his peeps lived in Egypt for more than four hundred years, and, as Egyptians, that is the language they knew and spoke. By the time of King David's coronation (ca. 993 BCE), Hebrew was finally coming online, but it took another two or so centuries before it became extant. There is nothing in the whole of the Torah to tell of translation problems that arose, if any. No, the whole of the Torah was written and redacted before, during, or after the return from exile in the sixth century BCE.

2. Nowhere in the stories does it say Moses wrote the whole of the Torah. It boggles the mind to think Moses wrote with different styles using future language forms that were not possible at the time of his point of reference. He allegedly wrote of his death and what happened to his people afterward. I know the argument being hurled at me right now. "But God could have ordained it and caused Moses to know of these things!" I am sorry, but this is specious thinking. This is not the god of the Hebrew people, for Proverbs 27:1 says, "Don't brag about what will happen tomorrow, you don't really know what will happen then" (IBC). In this discussion, we want to have our cake and eat it too. Our hubris is such that we must invent reasoning that is spurious and suspect to even ourselves, if only we will admit it, which for two thousand years we have not.

3. Only once in the Torah does it speak about God telling Moses to write anything down. It was about a specific action against the Amalekites so the Israelites would remember God's curse upon the Amalekites. We find the story in Deuteronomy 31. However, what Moses was told to write is the Law (the Torah), which is a gloss.

> And Joshua mowed down the Am'alek and his people with the edge of the sword. And the LORD said to Moses, "Write this as a memorial in a book and recite it in the ears of Joshua, that I will utterly blot out the remembrance of Am'alek from under heaven." —Exodus 17:13-14 (RSV)

And Moses wrote this law and delivered it unto the priests,
the sons of Levi, which bare the Ark of the Covenant of the
LORD, and unto all the elders of Israel.
—Deuteronomy 31:9 (RSV)

It speaks to something about ancient writing, which is often forgotten because it does not fit the narrative of the twenty-first century. Fresh words had no weight. For centuries, it was not uncommon for something like Deuteronomy to be ascribed into the mouth of someone from a much earlier time, especially someone venerated in history. Who better than Moses to give this impressive work on the LAW, I ask.[2] To have the gravitas needed, we must have a powerful name attached to the book. Again, our hubris refuses to see misunderstanding between what was in this writing and the reality of *Sitz im Leben* in Exodus, Judges, 1 and 2 Samuel, and 1 and 2 Kings.

4. Now we get to the fun stuff. For millennia, we knew of no other writings from other cultures other than Egypt that existed corresponding to the supposed age of the Torah. However, in 1849, Austen Layard, an English archaeologist, found a fragmented piece of clay writing in the ruined library of Ashurbanipal at Nineveh.[3] That clay tablet contained what is now known as the Enuma Elish, a Babylonian creation myth. Following many years and archaeological discoveries, more and more copies of this epic creation story were discovered, and the story was rounded out. Words in this epic are Sumerian in origin, which indicates an even older beginning, from the early twenty-third century BCE. These include the names of Tiamat's monsters, Marduk's wind, and the name for man. The chief god in the epic is the Babylonian Marduk, and not the older Sumerian god, Enlil, pointing to its long history for this epic. This story has been, in its various forms, dated to as early as the nineteenth century BCE. Hammurabi even references this epic in his code.[4]

---

2   I have a real problem with the traditional view of the Torah being ascribed as the books of the law. There *is* law in the Torah, yes, but the real importance of the Torah is the word *instruction*.

3   King Ashurbanipal reigned from 669–631 BCE. His kingdom is known as the Neo-Assyrian Empire. Interested in ancient literary works, he amassed more than 100,000 texts and documents in his library. The Library of Ashurbanipal had no equal until the Library of Alexandria, centuries later.

4   The Code of Hammurabi, written in Akkadian (ca. 1755 BCE). Hammurabi was the sixth king of the First Dynasty of Babylon. The basalt stele on which the primary copy of the code is written was uncovered in 1901 in Susa (Iran). It is now located in the Louvre Museum.

Mesopotamian religion prior to Islam was long lived. Civilizations like Sumer, Akkad, Assyria, Babylonia, and Persia contributed to the mythology and god worship in the eighth century BCE when the Hebrews encountered them personally for the first time. The earliest evidence of the Mesopotamian state religion is from the mid-fourth millennium, when writing was being invented.[5] That is not surprising, for before writing, we have no permanent record. This is part of the arsenal used by those who subscribe to Bishop James Ussher's age of the world: "See, there is no written record prior to 4004 BCE, therefore we cannot know for certain humans were present!" Which is silly and should be laughed at.

Polytheism and personal relationships with the gods were at their peak throughout the world during the time of the exile (587–539 BCE) with Marduk being the chief god of the Mesopotamians.[6] Every year at the time of the annual flooding of the Tigris and Euphrates Rivers, a twelve-day celebration took place. Known as the Akitu, the occasion revolved around the end of death (winter) and new life beginning. The exiled Jews knew this festival and participated in the celebration. They had to, for a state mandate is something one obeys. One feature of the Akitu was the recitation of the *Enuma Elish*, the origin story in their worldview. The *Enuma Elish* was part of everyday life, even to those exiled to the lands of Babylon. Scholars know the first chapter of Genesis was written not by Moses but by a writer from sometime around the return of the Jews from exile in Babylon in the late sixth century BCE. When seeking someone who is a prolific and seasoned author of that time, we must consider Ezra. He was a trained scribe in Babylon and was part of the elite, both in Babylonian circles and in Jewish politics and religion. It is uncertain whether he penned his origin story during his time in Babylon or upon his time in Judah. Regardless, his goal was to present an origin story that showed, and proved, his god was greater than the gods of his erstwhile captors. Scholars comment on how similar the two creation stories (Hebrew and Babylonian) are. When either work is read, one's mind will be drawn to likenesses that evoke comparisons with the other. This chapter will not be exhaustive but will show how Ezra did yeoman's work in creating a piece of art for us to read millennia later with glee and awe.

---

5   Yes, millennium—6,000 years ago!

6   Marduk was also known as Bel. Remember this factoid when reading the addition in Daniel known as "Bel and the Dragon."

Ezra put his god outside of creation. This is our first major change from saga norms that appear. Suddenly, a Cosmic Creator God who cannot be manipulated by the forthcoming epic creation event is presented. By doing so, Ezra gained preeminence for his god over the gods of the *Enuma Elish*. This Cosmic Creator God spoke, and creation responded. In the *Enuma Elish*, the primordial gods were defined by creation itself and had to respond to events that came from the creation process. Ezra let there be chaos in the beginning, as deep and dark as in the *Enuma Elish*. He did not stop there, however. The Genesis god used the chaos as a warehouse of useful odds and ends to create order—and in a systematic process! Events are prosaic, as they occur in the calm and peace of the cycles of creation. The Hebrew god was pleased with everything that transpired.[7] Sadly, in the *Enuma Elish*, even though order was created, there is a transience built into it. We see it through the strife between the ordered things and the primordial gods. We find no sense of an overarching structure in the entire process in the *Enuma Elish*. By that, I mean we grasp no real order of the occurrences in any genuine sense. We cannot see any timeline or coherence of order. The Cosmic Creator God, in his first act, created a timeline structure. His "'Let There Be Light!'—and Light Is!"[8] is a testament to the subtlety of writing that today is only beginning to be understood or accepted.

Peace and tranquility reigned throughout the whole of Genesis 1. Everything created was good to the Cosmic Creator God's eye. In the *Enuma Elish*, we find disagreement, wars, squabbles and even a cosmos-wide battle of primordial gods fighting with their heirs. (Good news, primordial Tiamat lost to Marduk). In contrast, the Genesis creation story recounts creation as if the Hebrew god is picking what colors to paint the walls or which type of carpet he wants in which room. The sense and style of order in Genesis is not found in the *Enuma Elish*. Genesis 1 requires that something must happen before something else occurs. Land must separate from the waters before plants and trees are enlivened. Water must be free of land prior to the creatures of the deep. Not so in the *Enuma Elish*. Stuff came into being in a rather higgledy-piggledy fashion. Order from chaos was involved, but with

---

7   "God saw that it was good" (vv. 9, 11, 18, 24, 31).

8   Hebrew; the transliteration as read.

a constant redefining of roles for that order. Ezra, the consummate writer, also sends pugilistic uppercuts to the *Enuma Elish*, and with relish, I must add. Both examples, to us in the twenty-first century, do not have the punch that his peers saw and felt. We of our age do not see the subtle insult that is inherent to those of his time.

Let's consider some of these polemics inside the story.

1. On the fourth day, Ezra's Cosmic Creator God puts the "luminaries" in the sky. We find a bright one, a lesser one, and tiny ones, all with limited and specific jobs. Sermons by the thousands and forests of trees have been felled explaining the how, why, and *what*?! of placing the luminaries the day *after* the plants and growing things are told to do their thing and three days after declaring LIGHT![9] We need to understand Ezra's *Sitz im Leben*. To be more specific, we need to understand what he was thinking at the time of writing. Would you like to know the real reason for plants, trees, and bushes being placed before the luminaries? I warn you—simplicity is the key. It's hidden in plain sight, so obvious as to be unseen! Look at the following list. Lift the lid of your traditional thinking box, look outside, and consider what is similar or dissimilar to each of these items:

    - The Cosmic Creator God hovering over the chaos before giving birth to his creation
    - Light, earth from sky, land from water
    - Grass, herbs, trees—each bearing seeds of their own kind
    - Luminaries that move across the expanse above
    - Fish and birds to be fruitful and multiply
    - Beasts of the earth—cattle and creeping things (progeny is not stated, but inferred)
    - Man and woman—created in the Cosmic Creator God's own image, to be fruitful and multiply

---

9   What light is will be discussed further in the next chapter.

Consider two abilities in your search, two essential traits of living organisms: (1) mobility, and (2) reproduction. The Cosmic Creator God has both mobility and reproductive capability prior to the week's events. He must have both to give both to his creation. (On a metaphysical level, the Cosmic Creator God has neither. He is outside creation. What is outside, by definition, cannot be defined by what is inside.) Light, earth and sky, land and water have neither mobility nor reproductive ability. Grass, herbs, and trees reproduce but cannot move about. The luminaries are mobile but cannot re-create. Fish and birds are mobile and make babies, but they are tethered to the seas and sky, not the earth. An important distinction exists for the world of man and animals, for they are bound to the earth. Human life revolves around the earth and its inhabitants. Humans will eventually subdue the sky and seas, but they are not intrinsic to the story, as man cannot live in either space. Beasts of the earth—cattle and creeping things—can move about on land and reproduce, but they are missing a piece of the puzzle. That missing piece is being made in the Cosmic Creator's image, which we read is given only to humans. Man and woman are mobile and reproduce. The last creation gets a third benefit: being like the creator! Finally, there is a logic to why the creation events were in the order as listed. I told you, in plain sight and so obvious. I felt stupid when I finally got the import. Do you grasp my awe at the writer?

2. Marduk was the prime god, and, as the prime god, he was the sun god (although he also got Jupiter). He was mobile, very mobile. His consort, Zarpanitu—who later was equated with Ishtar and Ianna and other goddesses whose roles included fertility and the like—received the moon. The stars in so many religions and even to this day are relegated to the minor gods and mythical heroes who did wonderful things for the gods and peoples of the earth. Ezra shot straight, right into the heart of the opposing religion in his description and ordering. He relegated these celestial bodies into a minor, fourth-day role, and he refused to even give them

their common, nonreligious names! No sun, no moon, no stars, just luminaries in the firmament. Not naming something in those days reduced them to an even more insignificant status. What is in the skies are just objects, doing what the Cosmic Creator God told them to do.

3. Another shot to the *Enuma Elish* speaks against the battle for dominance between the primordial gods and Marduk. Sadly, over the following millennia, we see a dilution of the power of Ezra's words into a mere ghost of what he was conveying to his peers. Genesis 1:21 says the Cosmic Creator God prepared the "great monsters of the seas." Over time, the wording has diluted until our translations read a myopic "great/large sea creatures, big animals, and huge whales." *So what, you wonder. Captain Ahab thought Moby Dick was a monster!* No, Ezra was comparing his monsters of the seas to what were the terrible, primordial monsters unleashed by Tiamat in the *Enuma Elish* to battle Marduk. We find the monsters' names in other places of the Hebrew testament, echoes of the Mesopotamian saga. The names *Rahab* and *Leviathan* are observed in Isaiah and Job. The Psalms also refer to the epic battle. Our author, Ezra, is saying brazenly that HIS god created the sea monsters to suit HIS purpose as HE saw fit. In the book of Job, the god of that story tells Job of taking Leviathan out for walkies occasionally![10] This is Ezra's god, and his god is still around to this day, unlike Marduk and his cronies. You will also notice the sea monsters are not named, despite being categorized. Again, another way to subsume their importance.

4. Let us consider the creation of humanity in the *Enuma Elish* (Egyptian, Canaanite, Greek, and Roman religious structures align with this Mesopotamian premise). The lesser gods are tired of doing the menial work for the higher gods. They wanted to lie about, eat bon-bons, and watch soap operas too. To appease these lesser gods, Marduk killed the god Kingu, who was the consort of the primordial goddess Tiamat, who was the head of the army that

---

10   See Job 41.

opposed Marduk. When Kingu saw the opposing army, he fled the battlefield. When captured, Marduk had Enki, another god, execute Kingu and use his blood to create humans. Enki used Kingu's blood to mix with the dust of the ground. Out popped humankind (many humans actually) to do the drudgework for the gods. We get, finally, to the creation of man and woman. Here we have another rather déjà vu feeling in the comparison of the stories. The Cosmic Creator God's final act is the origin of male and female. He blessed them by saying, "Here you go. This that came before you is yours. Enjoy!" We of the twenty-first century take it to mean, and rightly so, that god formed order out of chaos for us. It is good to have pride in being the ultimate creation, and my god is okay with that pride.

I want to get metaphysical here for a moment. Please indulge me, for I see Ezra's god, the Cosmic Creator God, making the cosmos just for Adam and Eve. I do not get that limitation in the other epic. On a bigger scale, I see that Cosmic Creator God making the cosmos just for me, and also just for you. This Cosmic Creator God is so Cosmic Creator that he was, and is, able to make the cosmos tailored to each person living and also for everyone who has been alive. Prove me wrong. That is the god Ezra is writing about, and that is who he is delineating in his treatise (Genesis 1).

And now, we get to Ezra's penultimate stroke. Over time, the most important and devastating arrow into the heart of the Mesopotamian religions has been diluted into nothingness, but here is that finishing blow: the first requirement of the god Marduk for fighting Tiamat and her denizens was, if Marduk won, the other gods would acknowledge and crown him chief god. Marduk's second demand was for the other gods to build him a temple. This temple would be from where he would rule his dominion—and where the other gods would pay him honor, as was his due. This temple would be on the mountain Sapon, to the far north of Mesopotamia. From there, Marduk would keep the peace, bless the earth, and plan for a world that suited him. The Hebrew story took one look at that idea and went cosmic. The Cosmic Creator God created the *earth* as his temple. Truer still, that same god created the cosmos as his domain to rule! Even bigger, that god created man and woman, not as savages, but as beings who are in communication with him, and he with them.

Ouch. Take that, Marduk, with your puny temple on the wrong side of the tracks!

Since Ezra wrote this story, the focus has shifted from Ezra's main point. We evangelicals are much to blame. We stop and proclaim humanity is the reason and purpose for the stuff that has gone on. My life up to this point revolved around accepting this as the purpose of Genesis 1. Creation was for man and woman, end of story. Of course, humanity is the best, for we are last created, and we have a stake in that storyline! How dare we even consider there might be more to the story? Humanity is the best of the best (of the best). However, this is not on Ezra's radar. Yes, he put humanity at the end—to show that humans are not meant to be the drudges of the gods, to do their scutwork. The Cosmic Creator God, who controls the entire cosmos with a mere word, put Adam and Eve (man and woman) and all who come from the earth on a higher level than the rest of creation. This is obvious from the writings in both testaments. That is not Ezra's end goal, lest we forget. From the very first words of his epic, Genesis 1, Ezra's god had dominion over every part of the cosmos. What the Cosmic Creator God did on those six days was to build his temple.

> And God saws everything that he had made and behold, it was very good. And there was evening and there was morning, a sixth day. —Genesis 1:31 (RSV)

This, my friends, is the end goal the Creator God had for the creation of the heavens and the earth. He was choosing to build his temple not from the labors of lesser beings, and not on some far-flung mountain, but upon the entire world, sky, and luminaries. Each fish, bird, animal—even the creepy-crawly ones. Yes, the great sea monsters were, and are, part of his temple. Every life, human included, is asked but one thing, to declare Ezra's god *the One*. Every living thing is programmed to do that. Why are we humans, the apex of the Cosmic Creator God's working, so obstinate? Ezra experienced another god and knew his god was so much different. Ezra enlightened his people of the truth. I am in awe of how Ezra put so much in so few words. And his words, if seen through his eyes, are as fresh today as when he wrote them.

I stand outside in the morning here in Tucson, and watch the sky brighten against the Rincon mountains and marvel at the temple of the Cosmic Creator God. Yes, I know the physics of how the sun's ejecta brings light and understand the science behind the dimming of the stars at dawn, but I still marvel at the ever-changing colors of the clouds as the sun prisms through them. And I think to myself, "What a wonderful world!"

CHAPTER 3

Looking Under the Hood

The first words of Genesis are also the Hebrew word for this work. That word is *bereshit*. *Genesis* is the Latin transliteration of the Greek word meaning "origin." To take the first few words of the saga as the title was a familiar concept of those times, especially in ancient times. If I were to say the opening line, "Space, the final frontier," you recognize the show being referenced is *Star Trek*. *Bereshit* is doing the same thing for the audience of the author's day.

We only have to look at the *Enuma Elish*, the Mesopotamian creation saga, to see the similarity. "When on high," is what *enuma elish* means. Our creation story is in Genesis. Genesis is a Greek word—the meaning is to be ignored here. In Hebrew, the creation story is found in *Bereshit*, which means "In the beginning." Below are the opening lines from the *Enuma Elish* and the book of Genesis. Notice the similarities and the differences.

> When (*enuma*) on high (*elish*) the heaven had not been named, Firm ground below had not been called by name, Naught but primordial Apse, their begetter, And Mummu Tiamat, she who bore them all, Their waters commingling as a single body, No reed had been planted, no marsh land had appeared.[1]

> In the beginning (*bereshit*) of God's creating the skies and the earth—When the earth had been shapeless and formless, and darkness was on the face of the deep, and God's spirit was hovering on the face of the water.[2]

---

1   Ephraim A. Speiser, trans. *Enuma Elish*, Tablet 1.
2   Richard Elliot Friedman, 2003, *The Bible with Sources Revealed*, HarperOne.

I find it amusing when preachers do their thing in Genesis. I have heard sermons, countless sermons, revolve purely around the first three words. If one is going to begin at the beginning of something, isn't saying, "In the beginning" the most succinct way to state that? Should we rather consider those words to be the title or description of what the story is about to unfold? Genesis 1, we are told, is an origin story that is millennia old, older than we can comprehend. Tradition says this cosmic commencement was ages old before it was written twenty-five centuries ago.

A close reading will take us into a framework of how to consider what is found in that chapter. I am sure you have heard them preached time and again. These theologies are rather convoluted and require leaps of logic and faith that we are forced to accept before proceeding to the desired understanding. After pondering a few, we will then consider a different path that makes sense of what is written. Along the way, a single thought needs to be held, and arguments must be compared to this idea: *the Cosmic Creator God likes form, function, and simplicity.* The world we occupy ought to make sense in our reasoning. If an idea is errant and appears out of place with another, the thought process is errant and needs to be reconsidered. All successful epics fit together and make sense. The tales will touch something inside us, for therefore, they are worthy. The stories do not need to be seamless, but coherent, and everything that is needed is found inside the tale. One needs to remember when reading these stories that our twenty-first-century mindset is incorrect. We are not the intended target. The people who were in the audience were the people of the age when they were first told or written. Those ancient people know well the background and preconceptions residing inside those tales. These ancient stories are filled with references to outside the influences of their time; theological, societal, and historical. If we rely solely on what is in Genesis, we miss the subtlety of what were, dare I say it, attacks on other ways of belief that were present throughout those days. There are three dichotomous camps regarding the linearity and supposed science of Genesis 1.

First, we have the literalists, the young earth (YE) believers. According to this approach, each and every word in the Bible is true and, therefore, there is only one meaning. The world was created in six days. There's nothing more to say, end of discussion. If you disagree with this, you are a hateful pagan who will roast in hell forever, no matter if you read the Bible, pray, and convert sinners by the thousands. These literalists refuse to look at our natural world and see the dichotomy of what is read and what has been discovered via the advancements of the age of the earth and the cosmos. This literalist cult has even invented a whole new "science" bent on making reality fit into their literal worldview. The means must justify the end, as defined by them. As a result, we have a stupid, ongoing fight about science being antibiblical or vice versa. The literalists even created a new set of religious laws that must be obeyed and agreed upon (I refer to the Chicago Statement on Biblical Inerrancy published in 1978). I have read through this screed so you do not have to, but it is online if you wish to peruse it yourself. This errant way of thinking is causing people to fall away from getting to know the Cosmic Creator God. I want to throw up in my mouth every time I read through it.

Second, we have the opposite side of the coin. This ideology is the old earth (OE) belief. Today's science tells us that the words in Genesis 1 are not as the YE belief system demands. OE considers what is written as an urban legend. OE ignores the older, proper definition of *myth*, which is how Genesis 1–11 ought to be viewed.[3] OE believes the whole of the creation story is false and must be ignored—a silly story made up by backward people who knew nothing. These people look down on the literalists as poor folk who need to be put away and fed pablum. They join in the Bible-versus-science fight with vigor, but from the other point of view. You will know these people by their beginning apology that starts, "But science says . . ."[4]

A third party is available, because we need a middle man, a fence-sitter. This idea, the gap theory (GT), mediates between the other two factions. However, they make up, out of whole cloth, a rationale by creating a story between two verses early in chapter 1. Sadly, GT attempts to arbitrate the differences, but does nothing except annoy the other sides with their fantastical idea. GT uses

---

3   The *American Heritage Dictionary* defines *myth* as "A traditional, typically ancient story dealing with supernatural beings, ancestors, or heroes that serves as a fundamental type in the worldview of a people, as by explaining aspects of the natural world or delineating the psychology, customs, or ideals of society."

4   Transparency time here. For the longest time, I was an old earther, but I have put aside my infantile ways for the better.

the English translations of Genesis 1:1–2 and inserts what is seen to be a way to mix the OT and YE theories together.[5] However, if you consider the Hebrew (original writing), and attempt to impose this GT concept, you are shot down because the Hebrew does not allow for the concept in shape, manner, or form.

Each of these belief systems contains holes in their logic and causes endless debate about their inability to fit their narrative to the real world. Chico Marx is famous for having once said, "Who are you going to believe, me or your own eyes?" If we are to assume the Cosmic Creator God does not create falsehoods, then the problems that crop up in their logic mean the proper questions are not being asked that allow for an answer that works, one that takes both theology and science into account.

Another problem that crops up among Christians is the overarching thought that the Cosmic Creator God made everything from nothing. This is called *ex nihilo* (from nothing). Everything about Genesis 1 must be read through this lens; it must not be deviated from. This is the only tangible way for their god to do his six-day miracle. The origin of this whole *ex nihilo* was formed as an opposition to various Christian gnostic (heretical) beliefs. Ex nihilo cannot be found anywhere, in either testament. It is made up. When reading the Genesis origin story, one finds that the *ex-nihilo* idea implodes. Does this matter in the long run of the story? For many, it destroys the whole of the Bible, for if the first chapter is not the truth, then nothing else is truth. This idea is silly and must be put aside, much like Yankees fans.

Listed below are the actions of each day of creation found in Genesis 1.

- **Day 1:** Creates (light)
- **Day 2:** Separates (waters above from waters below)
- **Day 3:** Separates/calls forth (land from waters, plants from the land)
- **Day 4:** Places, but does not name (luminaries in the firmament [sky])
- **Day 5:** Calls forth (fish and birds)
- **Day 6:** Calls forth/makes (land animals, man and woman)
- **Day 7:** Rests

---

5   Google "gap theory" for an explanation.

I see no *ex nihilo* except (possibly) on the first day. So let us consider that day further. In the preamble to the actual creation goings-on, we see the Creator God contemplating the world before doing anything. I am reminded of several large projects I have done. The building supplies are present, the tools are laid out, and the work list is evaluated one more time. Here in this creation story, before the first cut is made or the first shovelful dug, there is one last moment of thought—and perhaps a deep breath—by the Cosmic Creator God. Verse 2 speaks to this where it mentions the "Spirit of God fluttering on the face of the waters." Even the Cosmic Creator God did one last check prior to doing his thing—whatever that is to be. This must mean the world, our blue marble in space, was already formed, although in total chaos and anarchy. So *ex nihilo* is, from the outset, not in play, nor can it be allowed anywhere in this chapter.

The first day is where confusion reigns supreme. If the Cosmic Creator God is a god of consistency and logic and simplicity, that day makes no sense when considering what followed. Questions arise. God created light, but the light sources were created on day four? What is this light, exactly? Why start with light? And most excellent questions they are! Before 1921, explanations of this light were varied. The most common answer says that the essence of the Cosmic Creator God is the mere requirement for light.[6] Talmudic passages say the luminaries were created on the first day, but only placed in the firmament on the fourth day. Some Christians claim it is the possibility of the Christ's (Jesus of Nazareth's) coming. This idea, popularized in early Christian circles, is still around today. Still others argue the earth did not begin rotating until the fourth day. Nice try in the logic department, but even through a theological lens, none of these theories pass the sniff test.

We are still on the hunt for an answer to the question of the light, so many turn to science for an answer. (I will go to my grave arguing there is no science in the Genesis 1 account of creation.) Science is bulwark for the above-mentioned fight clubs. All three fight clubs are incorrect; the first two are onto something—although in different directions—but are too entrenched to admit their errors. YE is confident the words are true, and this is true, but

---

6   This is known in theological circles as Shekinah glory. *Shekinah* means "the presence of YHWH."

not in the way demanded by them. OE says today's science is correct. Again, true, but not the way they think. Look at the list above. The proof of both ideas is there in plain sight. But what is the obvious key they both miss? And why am I lying when I say with confidence that there is no science?

Until 1900, no genuine answer was forthcoming to our question of light. That is, not until Albert Einstein did a paper circa 1905, which defined what had been missing up to that point. He defined the concept of *space-time*. What was created on day one of the creation story? Space and time. Here is how the science works (notice no math is involved): it is a pure logic pursuit. From our earliest days, we are told we live in a three-dimensional world. Length, width, and height are the requirements for anything that is physical. However, Einstein said a piece was missing. The missing piece was location. That location depends on its relative location to the observer. That location has infinite possibilities of places to be at *any given moment*. And there we see time involved: "any given moment."[7] Everything physical is located relative to everything else relative to when it is being considered. For a physical object to exist, it must be located somewhere, and that somewhere must be located in time. That, my friends, is why light got first billing. When we consider the response to the order, "Let there be light," time is reflected in the ordering of days. Time is the original *order from chaos* in the story. The Creator God had to have *time* before doing anything *physical*. Twenty-five hundred years ago, a nonscientist beat Albert Einstein to the punch! However, this discovery is proved by science. The original idea is a logical thought process.

The common explanation for why the Cosmic Creator God did the thing he did was to create order from chaos. I agree with that notion, but it is vague, and that irritates me. We need to understand the metaphysical meanings of *chaos* and *order* to get into the brilliance of the author's intentions. This is a point when we need to go extrabiblical to get a better view of what was going on in the author's world at that time. In other world religions, the gods were, themselves, part of the creation cycle and subject to creation's happenings. Order came from things being separated into two distinct roles. Sweet water

---

7   I know this is very simplistic. I do not include where the observer is located, nor do I care to discuss gravity's involvement.

was distinguished (separated) from salty water. Two gods appeared as beings who took their personas from those roles. I use roles because of what they were—their interaction among everything else that was, or would be, created. The major thrust of the separation/definition process was to give a name to that specific manifestation. A name gave it reality. Reality gave that created object its power and role in life. To give a part of reality, a name gave the person/god power over the additional part of reality. With me so far? I realize this is metaphysical to the extreme, but we must understand this underlying principle before we go further.[8]

Let us consider an example of clarification. Honest Sally Inc. has a research department. The head researcher presents a widget to the board and says, "We could make a killing with this new widget!" To which Sally herself asks, "What is it and what does it do?" The marketing department's reply (and this is key), is "We have not named it yet because we do not know what it does." Right there, the idea dies a sudden death. Another example will show the contrast. The TV sitcom *Home Improvement* had a schtick where the two hosts would introduce a new product from the show's sponsor. "Introducing the Binford 6100!" To the show's viewers, it mattered not what the product was, but the name Binford 6100 was the identifier needed. By using those two words, we knew an idea presented was for our enjoyment. The power of a name in real life! In other creation stories, the name of the god was given by the role defined by the new reality. The gods, therefore, were defined by creation. Naming the role was a byproduct of that creation. Also, power ranking is the god's importance to the sum of the whole. A god of a small stream is nothing compared to the storm god or the goddess of fertility.

Now we turn to the Hebrew creation story. The Cosmic Creator God is outside the creation. He is not influenced by the creation; rather, he influences the creation. He separates, defines, and names the results. His word is the driver for what occurs. Nothing occurs without his say-so. We see the Cosmic Creator God responsible for naming the process or object, and that naming defines its function. If translations were clearer, we'd grasp this in the directive to the grasses. Our English translations say:

---

8   I gnash my teeth with frustration regarding such topics—perhaps it need not be taught from the pulpit, but this stuff is what should have been taught in Sunday school.

And God said, "Let the earth put forth vegetation, plants yielding seed, and fruit trees bearing fruit in which is their seed, each according to its kind, upon the earth." And it was so. —Genesis 1:11 (RSV)

The Hebrew transliteration is *Let the grass grass!* Oh, what we miss from not being able to read the original language! The name defines its function. The name-giver provides the power to fulfill its function, its role. Words cannot offer the full import of an idea, in Hebrew or English. Here is a perfect example. The writer, twenty-five hundred years ago, did his best. Yet his best is insufficient for us to understand what is being offered. I am sure some of my readers will grasp my attempt to delineate what is to come. Others will need to ponder what is written to grasp the real meaning. Here is the passage in Genesis 1 to which I refer:

The earth was without form and void, and darkness was upon the face of the deep; and the Spirit of God was moving over the face of the waters. — Genesis 1:2 (RSV)

Ezra is doing his best here to tell us something. For us to know what he is speaking of, we must first understand an empirical fact, which, on its face, appears obtuse. As seen in the examples above, to name something, one must first know what it is, and the most direct way to that knowledge is to compare it to something else. Ezra uses the words *water, form, void,* and *darkness.* These words fail since, in their placement, we have no objective reference to define those words. We of today know their opposites. So, too, did Ezra's peers, however, they understood what was being offered. What was being offered was what we know as nothing.[9]

Ezra is doing his best to tell us from a metaphysical viewpoint that there is no chaos yet. For nothingness cannot be chaotic. Chaos needs to have an opposite to compare against. Consider the verse above carefully: there is nothing there. The writer had no words to operate with, and so his attempt is weak, for he had to use words—his best words—to give a picture of the infinite nothing. We see him failing as he uses *darkness* prior to darkness being created. His use of the word *waters* is another weak attempt to

---

9   Sadly, the logic stream demands of us that when defining *nothing*, we are actually creating a *something*. This is where Ezra floundered.

emphasize a massive nothingness. His term, *the earth,* is meant only to show a focal point that was to become. The author is attempting to give his hearers and readers a mere inkling of what *was* prior to it becoming *something.*[10] Yet the writer tells us there was something—something outside the nothingness. The Cosmic Creator God is present outside the nothingness. His presence, the Spirit, knows what the writer knows. If we stop and think, we know as well—although that understanding is difficult to grasp. Simply rename the nothing. *There is nothing. Yet, if there is nothing, everything is possible. The Spirit of the Cosmic Creator God is hovering over what is possible.*[11]

The Cosmic Creator God then puts the possible into existence. Possibility is not chaos, but potential.[12] What is possible is without limit, as we see in the next set of verses as creation takes place. From nothing comes something. There is no *ex nihilo,* for the substance used is what was possible. Such things are not spoken from the pulpit, nor taught in Sunday school. Nothing like this is opined upon by theologians or philosophers of any faith. What we get instead are sermons detailing each and every tiny, irrelevant, and often wrong tidbit about the six days of creation. Ezra tells of the Cosmic Creator God starting the clock and then separating and defining roles for the rest of the creation—from what is possible! We are so invested in getting to the sixth day; tradition tells us that day is the proper end of the story, that the best for last was on the sixth day when humans came on the scene. Huzzah! Pastors and theologians bow and step off the stage to wild applause. And we miss the jaw-dropping and humbling impact these few words contain.

> Then the heavens and the earth were completed, and all their array, And God completed on the seventh day the task He had done, and He ceased on the seventh day from all the tasks he had done. And God blessed the seventh day and hallowed it, for on it he had ceased from all his tasks that he had created to do. This is the tale of the heavens and the earth when they were created. —Genesis 2:1–3 (Robert Alter's English Translation)

According to the writer, day seven is the climax, not day six (sorry for treading on preachers' toes). For a better understanding of this truth,

---

10   Do not get me wrong. I have the highest admiration and respect for Ezra. His masterful handicraft leaves me breathless with wonder.

11   *Cambridge Dictionary* defines *possible* as "Able to be done or achieved, or able to exist."

12   *Cambridge Dictionary* defines *potential* as "Possible when the necessary conditions exist."

imagine you have purchased a house. As you walk inside, you see the freshly painted rooms with carpeting laid and brand-new appliances in place. As you wander through the rooms, you appraise the potential for where the furniture is to be placed, which rooms the kids will have, where the dining table will sit, where your comfy chair will go, and how life will be in this new abode. The moving truck appears as your family and friends arrive to drag the furniture in, put the dishes and toys in their proper places—just as you planned. After the work is done and the required pizza and beverages are consumed, you stop, breathe a sigh of relief, and stop to rest, never to do anything again.

Or do you? The best part of the move is now! You get to live and create a life in this house, making it a home. Are you resting from creating your home? Yes, absolutely! But the creation work is past, your house is set up according to how you created it. Living (resting) is now the present and the future. Here is where the rest of the story begins. We now have a basis, a roadmap, to understand how the rest of Genesis, the whole of the rest of the Tanakh, will unfold. This is the glory of the first origin story: the Cosmic Creator God was creating his home—or, more accurately, his sacred space, for we know from this story he did the cosmos as well.

One last thought and we will be done with this creation story. We put the debate of science versus theology to bed. There is no science in this story; there never was—only clear-headed logic. We are the poorer for spending the effort to shoehorn science into places where it does not need to be. Our universe is 13.7 billion years old. Our blue marble called earth is 4.5 billion years old. We are made of stardust. The Cosmic Creator God is not afraid of our increasing knowledge, for his creation is out there for all to see. All we have to do is look and look well at the surrounding creation right in front of our faces—and of the possibilities that await!

CHAPTER 4

The Garden of Eden

The second creation story is known by several names. "Adam and Eve," "The Garden of Eden," and "The Fall" are the most common. What is found in this story as read is much older than the first creation epic found in Genesis 1. Here is where actual oral traditions that date far back into time are found. At least four origin stories are pasted together to form the whole, with two noticeable later redactions. The name of the god is personalized, which is different from the generic name as seen in the first creation story.[1] Attention is focused here not on *how* stuff was created but *why* stuff was created. To help us understand what is going to happen, we must first consider who and when this saga was put to paper. Finding this information will allow us to gain insight into the *Sitz im Leben* for this story. When was it put to paper? This is the first question that will point us to the person. Archaeology is our guide here. There are those who demand that the Torah and the histories were done in the time of King David while he brought the two nations together under one rule. The United Kingdom (Israel to the north and Judah to the south) was, in reality, a small backwater group of disparate clan structures who were conquered and joined by a powerful ruler, David. Archaeology has determined no record of writing or record-keeping found during David's or Solomon's reigns.[2] We do not find widespread literacy and record-keeping

---

1   Chapter 1 uses *Elohim* (the god). Chapter 2 uses *Yahweh Elohim* (the god's personal name).

2   King David's reign began ca. 1000 BCE. Solomon's reign followed.

until King Omri's time.[3] There is no sign of translation issues that indicate original writings in another language in the writings of Genesis during the United Kingdoms' time.

Histories, poetry, and philosophical writings did not appear until the late eighth century BCE. For our discussion, archaeology and linguists break the time frame down into three divisions: pre-exile, exile, and post-exile.[4] Political storm clouds (the Assyrian Empire expansion plan) portending the future drove these pre-exile writers to create permanent records of their history in anticipation of the future, which was certain, although not welcome. Tradition says Moses wrote the first five books, and the prophet Samuel wrote the histories.[5] These two men hold the titles only by tradition but are suspect since they both died early in the storylines and therefore had no logical way to know the future. Are we left with no knowledge, then, of who penned these books? Well no, not with absolute assurance. Two people stand out in the crowd, however: Baruch ben Neriah, a pre-exile writer of note, who was also Jeremiah the prophet's scribe, and Ezra, a post-exile scribe and political leader. Both are noted writers during their times. Baruch is the best candidate for the pre-exile period and is known for his penmanship and writing style during this time. His ability to write wonderful stories is legend, as we will see. He was alive and active during King Josiah's reign[6] when the Deuteronomic text was "found" and read to the king, which caused a massive upheaval to the theocratic way of life in Israel.

Scholars have described the writings of the Torah and Joshua, Judges, 1 and 2 Samuel, and 1 and 2 Kings as the Deuteronomic texts for their coherent linearity of purpose. Richard Elliot Friedman, the noted Old Testament scholar, points to Baruch as the most likely person to have penned Deuteronomy through 1 and 2 Kings, and I agree.[7] I see his signature style in much of the Torah as well. So we have our original person who put all the divergent oral stories into a workable whole. That takes care of the original workings. But there are many places in Baruch's various works where the

---

3   Ca. 880 BCE.

4   Pre-exile ca. 750–586 BCE. Exile ca.586–539 BCE. Post-exile ca. 539–332 BCE.

5   This is a mistake that will be discussed further in another chapter.

6   Circa 640–609 BCE.

7   Richard Elliot Friedman, 1997, *Who Wrote the Bible?*, HarperOne.

story has discordant turns, as if someone stuck a gloss or commentary into Baruch's storyline. Two books found in the Torah, Leviticus and Numbers, do not appear to have Baruch's touch and are reminiscent of Ezra's style. We know also that Ezra was well versed in writing since he had been trained at the highest levels in Babylon for such purposes. He has two books ascribed to him, Ezra and Nehemiah. There is another book known as 2 Esdras, a noncanonical book that is revered by both Jewish and early Christian scholars alike, which must be considered. In 2 Esdras, we find that Ezra and forty other scribes had to rewrite the entire Tanakh because it had been severely damaged during the destruction of the temple at the start of the exile. The redactions and additions show Ezra's style of writing, so we now know how the last pieces were put into place. Two of the redactions found here in the Garden story that point to Ezra are the insertion of the rivers of Eden and the removal of the celebration of the union of Adam and Eve (the sex part) for reasons described later.

What was the *Sitz im Leben* to cause the desire for a permanent record of the Hebrew people? The Assyrian Empire was expanding its borders in a dramatic fashion during the eighth century, intending to invade and conquer Egypt. To do so, they had to go right through Canaan to get to their goal. The Northern Kingdom, Israel, was in the way, literally, since they controlled the main highway into Egypt. Starting around 732 BCE, Tiglath-Pileser III started capturing and deporting city populations throughout Canaan. Finally, in 702 BCE, the Northern Kingdom's capital of Samaria was captured and the deportation that became known as the Ten Lost Tribes occurred. Political stuff happened right about then, which caused the Assyrians to return home before ending Judah's tenure. Realists in the Southern Kingdom knew they were next to go when the Assyrians came around again.[8] Now we know when and by whom. The original compilation was written prior to the exile to have a permanent record of the history of the children of Israel, if that people were dissolved by an invader. Our writers, both accomplished and able, took the role of record-keeping and did a masterful job with their attempt.

---

8   I know 2 Kings 19 says Yahweh's angel kicked the rear of the Assyrian army, who fled from their siege of Jerusalem. However, Assyrian history dates two major outbreaks of civil unrest near Nineveh, their capital, which forced the army to return.

> Now no shrub of the field had yet grown on the earth, and no plant of the field had yet sprouted, for the Lord God had not caused it to rain on the earth, and there was no man to cultivate the ground. Springs would well up from the earth and water the whole surface of the ground.
> —Genesis 2:5–6 (NET)

Imagine a desert wasteland. No, not what is outside my house in southern Arizona, but the Sahara Desert or the Gobi Desert. That is what we are led to think of in this passage. But as our compiler knows, this opening statement will become important at the end of the story! These two verses are packed with sweet, rich, gooey goodness, which is ignored all too often. We read the land is barren of any greenery and there is no precipitation. Not so. The Hebrew defines the shrub of the field being *wild unwanted plants*, and the plant of the field as being *cultivated grains*. These cultivated grains refer to any type of grain that is used for making bread: oats, corn, barley, spelt, rye. The other plants referred to are any type of weed that grows along and with those grains.

Follow the logic here. There were no weeds because there was no rain. There were no cultivated grains because there was no human to tend to them. Grain, weeds, and rain must be integral to the story somewhere to be mentioned at the very start of the story. It is, for the "curse" and expulsion of Adam will bring these items back to our minds. What does that imply, then? Tradition gets this wrong. At the start of the story, the world is empty—of weeds and cultivated grains. Grass, trees, saguaros, no-fruit-bearing shrubberies were present and growing quite nicely. We all know trees and all sorts of bushes grow without rain. I look out my windows and see a myriad of cactus and trees and bushes of all types doing their thing. So much flora covers the terrain that the ground is hidden from view, and this is in the Sonora Desert where the rain is most certainly a rare occurrence. Peers of the writers knew this as fact, so they understood the face of the earth was not Sahara-like, just missing some stuff.

How cool is that?!

> The Lord God (*Yahweh Elohim*) planted an orchard in the east, in Eden; and there he placed the man he had formed. The Lord God (*Yahweh Elohim*)

made all kinds of trees grow from the soil, every tree that was pleasing to look at and good for food. (Now the tree of life and the tree of the knowledge of good and evil were in the middle of the orchard.) —vv. 8–9 (NET)

Eden is most commonly called the Garden, but reading what comes next describes the place as an orchard. Trees that are fruit-bearing. Nothing about bushes or plants that are edible, just trees. Here we now add the fruit-bearing bushes and plants and tubers to the outside world, making that place an even richer environment than before. In the time of writing this story, imaginations pictured date palms, olive trees, pomegranates, almonds, and figs.

Was this orchard created in an instant? Did Yahweh Elohim snap his celestial fingers and poof, it was done? Was there an enclosure around to secure the borders? We know there was a gate from later verses, but again, some questions are not meant to be asked since such things are not mentioned by the writer. The name for the orchard is often referred to as Eden. *Eden* in Hebrew means "pleasure." Pleasure, or, according to some scholars, "paradise," tells the readers of that time of a place of security and peace and enjoyment. Such wording is to be compared to what is outside the orchard, an unsecured place where there is a harsh environment, just like most of the Ancient Near East (ANE). People today are right to think of an oasis as an example.

Now a river flows from Eden to water the orchard, and from there it divides into four headstreams. The name of the first is Pishon; it runs through the entire land of Havilah, where there is gold. (The gold of that land is pure; pearls and lapis lazuli are also there). The name of the second river is Gihon; it runs through the entire land of Cush. The name of the third river is Tigris; it runs along the east side of Assyria. The fourth river is the Euphrates. —vv. 10–14 (NET)

Many good-hearted people believe the garden will be found by interpreting what is written. That is, with the supposed wealth of information given, all one has to do is decipher the words, get past the two cherubs and their flaming, rotating swords, and grab an apple. (I am sure there is no thought of selling the fruit of the tree of life or making a tourist trap in their minds in the least). Let us consider what is written about the location in the story.

First, the garden was created in the east (see v. 8)—precisely where in the east is not mentioned. One must first consider if the garden is to the east of Canaan. Then, if one is honest, the Mesopotamian region must come next, for that is where the most ancient of "history" comes from. However, are we going to be literal and look in a cardinal direction? How far to the east will one have to go? Anyone who considers a map will soon realize that they must go north before heading east if one is to get to the locations of where the original oral traditions started. That place is in the Caucus Mountains. Or one will look far to the south and east, where the most ancient of cities are. Eridu, Uruk, Ur, Larsa, and Lagash are obvious choices if one heads that way. Neither of these directions are suitable for us. Directly east of Canaan is an even harsher desert, which was impassable at that time and is still rugged today.

East of *what* is not defined in the story, nor is it intended to be. *East* must be considered in ancient metaphysical terms. In ancient times, cardinal directions did not point toward geographical places but are related to intentions. More to the point, those are intentions based on what the future foretells. East is toward a future, brightening with hope. Why? The sun rises with a fresh day's future to unfold! This is obvious; anyone who gets up early enough to watch the sunrise knows the day brightens in the east. YHWH sets his garden in the east—the promise of a future with his planned creation, humanity. The exact location is where hope and love and communion are planned.

We must now consider the elephant in the room when it comes to location. There is much time spent talking about the Rivers Pishon and Gihon for some reason. Literalists insist these rivers must be connected to each other and, if so, they will mark where the garden is located. Wishful thinking, for here is our first taste of Ezra's hand in the story.

The Tigris and Euphrates Rivers are known, no problem there. It is the two other rivers, the Pishon and the Gihon, that are questionable. Upon research, these names are assigned to any of several rivers. I have seen the Nile and the Jordan, which once extended down to the Red Sea, offered as candidates. In Mesopotamia proper, the Wadi al-Batin and the

Karun River are in the conversation. The Ganges and Indus are also in contention, since why not?

This makes the location of the land called Havilah (which is important for our consideration here) at opposite ends of the earth. Is Havilah in Egypt, or India? Another possibility is closer to home at the delta of the Persian Gulf.

Geographically, nothing works, so cosmology is out. Now what to do? Well, it's super easy—barely an inconvenience. How many rivers are mentioned? Four. How many cardinal points are there? Four. With this in mind, we will take a slight detour and consider temples at that time. Temples were not merely sacred spaces but the actual residence of a god. So, too, the Garden of Eden is Yahweh Elohim's temple. Temples were aligned according to the cardinal points, considering seasonal sun, moon, and star alignments. This is to represent the god being over all the earth. Temples in the Ancient Near East depicted rivers originating from inside, depicting waters of life springing from the god's beneficence to his people.[9] In our story, we have four rivers—four rivers that water the entire earth. That is what the rivers meant to this construction we read in the second creation story.

One last point to be made here of the rivers—the river Pishon is supposed to run through the entire land of Havilah. As discussed above, its location is up for grabs. What is important is what is found there. Gold, pearls, lapis lazuli, bdellium, and onyx are mentioned, depending on which translation you read. Look back at the tree comments. Such riches are found in the ground, not hanging or growing from trees. This is a direct shot across the bow of the Babylonian mythos. The Gilgamesh epic describes trees that grew such baubles. People of that age got the connection. It is *not* intended to be a literal location. A temple faces the bright future, with water and food for sustainability and jewels that are found in their proper places. This is what Ezra is saying. He was familiar with what was being said in other lands and cared enough to insert his side of the story as an update.

> And out of the ground, Jehovah God (*Yahweh Elohim*) formed every beast of the field, and every bird of the heavens; and brought them unto

---

9   Most times, the river was shown as reliefs on the walls. Rivers and lush plant life abounded on the walls of the entryway into the temple. Occasionally, there was actually a waterway that flowed out of the temple.

the man to see what he would call them: and whatsoever the man called every living creature, that was the name thereof. And the man gave names to all cattle, and to the birds of the heavens, and to every beast of the field. —vv. 19–20 (ASV)

Adam had been created prior to the garden being built. He was then put into the garden to tend it. I know people who like to be loners, but not Adam. With no one to talk to about the latest ball game or discuss how the stock market was doing, he got really lonely. Arguing with a date palm gets boring really quick, as we all know from experience.

Adam was given the charge of establishing dominion over the animals of the land and birds of the air. This is what we see here, the naming deed. This was done after the garden was created, so the assumption is that the naming act was performed inside the garden. It does not say so, but one must remember what happens when one assumes. Do you see anything about the two statements of the animals and birds that cause pause? Got it in one! There are no fish involved. Obviously, Yahweh Elohim did not create a large enough pond for Leviathan to swim about. (Moby Dick was practicing for his stint with King Ahab in a few millennia, but that is not intrinsic to the story.) Look at the listing of what Yahweh formed out of the ground. Specifically consider the wording used. "Of the field" is the terminology. We saw this term used above; however, we must invert the meaning for animals. Think about it this way, Old McDonald's farm is not where lions and tigers and bears (oh, my!) are located. We are talking about undomesticated animals. And birds were created. But when did Old McDonald's animals get created? I dunno. It does not say—and does it really matter?

However, when the naming time came about, the domesticated animals (cows, sheep, goats, and such) are the first to go through the line to be named. This delineation is the start of a naming hierarchy, for we see a purpose of division between animals. The order of importance is domesticated animals, our winged friends, and finally, the wild critters, which include all the creepy crawlies. All air-breathing animals are subject to the will of humanity. Some are more equal than others. Sorry folks, robber jays are more important than elephants. Cows are more important than that yummy turkey on

Thanksgiving. That is what we are learning here. Fish do not breathe air, nor inhabit the land. Therefore, they are not included in this origin story. As for the cattle, I feel comfortable in arguing they were created in the same manner and time frame as the rest of the garden. Either that, or some later scribe got hand cramps, and it was lost. Your choice.

This book is intended for anyone, teen or older, to read. With that in mind, this part will require finesse, for it deals with a subject that is verboten by any church or religious entity. In the rendering of this passage, there is no intent to offend. As best as possible, the wording will be G-rated, but there will be innuendos.

> But Adam found no perfect mate for himself. Therefore, the LORD God caused a heavy sleep to fall upon the man. And he slept. And he took one of his ribs and closed up the flesh in its place. And with the rib which the LORD God had taken from the man, he made a woman. And he brought her to the man. Then the man said, "This, now, is bone of my bones and flesh of my flesh. She shall be called 'woman', because she was taken out of the man." —vv. 20–23 (RGT)

For the first time in the story, the word *Adam* is referring to the person, not the morphic representation. This is surprising. Prior to this, and in the rest of the passage, when the word *Adam* is used, it refers to an androgynous being. Everything that happens after this shows Adam as man. A scribal error is the probable reason for this, and a deeper discussion on this is found in the next chapter. The important part of this story comes with what is stated in the last sentence. Here we find the androgynous *Ish* (man) speaking about the androgynous *Isha* (woman). Even though the two are standing face-to-face, the Hebrew states they are not as we know man and woman to be—yet. I call shenanigans on this. What we see here is a truncation, a redaction that is most likely Baruch keeping it G-rated. Yahweh Elohim did not do the work to present another being to the man for him to say something to the effect of, "Yeah, looks okay to me." Yahweh Elohim is a god, *the* God. He had a cosmic stereo system playing Barry White's best music as the woman was presented to the man. The man's response? Man's eyes bug out. Man's tongue drops out of his mouth. Man says, "Hubba, hubba! What a babe! Whoopee!"—or something to that effect. Do you get my drift? Also, what occurs naturally to humans occurred right then and there. And often afterwards.

Are you picking up what I am putting down? I am endeavoring so hard not to mansplain. This is a key point that is ignored and even disparaged in the Judeo-Christian religion. Yahweh Elohim is not stupid, nor does he do oopsies. When he made Adam and Eve, he was intentional in creating both male and female, down to the last detail. The Cosmic Creator God in the first creation story told male and female to *be fruitful and multiply! Fill the earth and subdue it!* History tells us other cultures joined in on the fun of being fruitful. Yes, far too often it was taken to the extreme, but that is not important for this conversation.

Tradition insists Cain and Abel were born outside the garden for the simple reason that Genesis 4:1 is the first time Adam and Eve were "intimate," and Cain was the result. With that in mind, and a whole pile of malarkey from the time of St. Paul, the idea of sex (there, I said it) and procreation was an anathema to religious thinking. St. Paul, bless his beady little heart, even said it would be better not to marry unless one was weak and not able to control themselves.[10]

Both the Cosmic Creator God and Yahweh Elohim have problems with that idea.[11] That is not, I repeat, *not* how or why man and woman were created. Yes, a high "body count" is full of potential problems. However, the church is (1) remiss in not teaching about sex, and (2) needs to stop with all the theological and moral baggage foisted upon kids. As a little league baseball coach, I spent many a happy hour working with kids to teach fundamentals and watched those same kids grow and have fun with their new skills. What is taught in churches about all the "begetting" is summed up like this: "Ew! You are going to hell if you do that!" And you adults—if you or your partner are not fully enjoying getting jiggy with each other, it's time for a reevaluation. God built you both with the tools to maximize the activity.

---

10   "To the unmarried and widows, I say that it is best for them to remain as I am. But if they do not have self-control, let them get married. For it is better to marry than to burn with sexual desire" (1 Corinthians 7:9, NET).

11   The Cosmic Creator God and Yahweh Elohim are one and the same. This will be discussed in a later chapter.

This chapter is built around the garden and its environment. What is above is stuff that is not referred to from the pulpit or from the lips of a Sunday school teacher. As said previously, this is pure gold! How much richer is the story with this savory background? Imagine knowing these details as the storyteller gifts your ears with what is written. All senses are heightened, and the story breathes with freshness each time. Good writing, Baruch and Ezra, you did fine! The next chapter will delve into other details that are more on the metaphysical spectrum. We will also see how our translations are too poor for the richness and, quite frankly, the pun-heavy intent of the writers. Foreshadowing is central, and in one case so obvious that it is invisible to the naked eye! How fun will that be?

CHAPTER 5

The "Fall"

Almost every Batman movie had a different director. Although the storylines vary, the real juice and appeal of the movies is how the director puts his own spin on the main character, Batman. Each movie follows the core tenants of Batman while inserting a unique taste and feel. Ezra and Baruch, in the first two creation stories, are of this same mold. *We have a god who prepares an environment for his ultimate creation, humanity.* This is the core value that is held through both stories. Our consideration in this chapter will first outline the major differences of the two creation stories and then dig into some juicy tidbits Baruch felt were important for his readers (and us) to know. As stated earlier, tradition tends to harmonize these two different creation accounts. I cannot see any relation between the two, other than the basic outline already mentioned. Here we will dig into some issues and compare potential problems. Again, I do not see a need for connectedness. These came from oral traditions. I have no problem with that thought.

Separate but Equal

The first story is *how* stuff got created. The second story is *why* it was created. This is our first separation. Ezra, in his cosmic creation, ends with "God saw all that he had made—and it was very good! There was evening, and there was morning, the sixth day." This last statement of the Cosmic Creator God does not ring true by the end of the second story? No, not in the least.

This brings us to the traditional thought that the second story must be only considered as day six, as in the first story. I have seen timelines that force everything that happened in the garden into a period of only twenty-four hours. Yeah, sure, pull my other leg, for it has bells on it. Even the intrepid Archbishop James Ussher demands this to be true.[1] By far, this idea is acknowledged as true since there is no mention of darkness. If we were to take this literally, then the whole of the second story had to occur in twelve to fourteen hours!

Here is the big problem with that idea. God *could* have made Adam and the garden in an instant—*boom!*—and done. For the god to create the animals and birds in an instant is possible, but getting Adam to name them as they walked or flew by in a conga line is going to take some time—a lot of time. Especially since the literalists insist the animals we know of today had to be present in the garden to be named. Which means the elephants, ostriches, beavers, dinosaurs, raptors, gorillas, camels (one hump or two) and (unladen) African or European swallows. I cannot imagine the time needed to name the creepy crawly things as well. All in a twelve-hour period. Come on, seriously?

Another dissimilarity that must be accounted for in this whole harmonization issue is that wonderful thing called *time*. Ezra, in his first account, makes time his first creation and everything after is based on this reality. We now know why. It was part of his polemical attack on the Babylonian creation account. Everything the Cosmic Creator God did was ordered, and, to do that, time must be involved so a reader knows exactly what occurred before and after something else.

Baruch ben Neriah did nothing of the sort in his account other than depict the god walking in the garden sometime during the day.[2] Translations fail here too. As read in the Hebrew, the order of origins is ambiguous. Which means

---

1   Archbishop James Ussher is the person responsible for the calculations, which demand the world was created starting in October of 4004 BCE. He and his magic calculator did this in the 1600s.

2   The Hebrew wording is indistinct. Both Jewish and Christian theologians differ widely on this account.

that despite what is read, we cannot be certain they actually happened in that order. For example, Adam was created first because humanity was the reason for the story. The garden was after Adam, although this does not sit well for a good ordering. Animals and birds before Eve is good only for the tension it gives to her creation. We also gather that childbirth was a known thing to humanity, as this is presented to Eve as a done deal that would only become harder in the future. A bit further on, we see Cain being extremely upset when he is exiled and forced to wander the earth. If not for being removed from the safety of the garden, why is his pain so great?

Where is an accounting for time found anywhere? From the opening description of the earth to when Adam and Eve were kicked out, we have no time frame to work from. God made man prior to creating the garden? How long did it take to create the garden? When exactly were Old McDonald's animals created? My ten-year-old grandson makes up better stories than the making of the animals before woman. Less than a day for the god to trip up his bestest creation and kick them out? Puhleeze.

The first creation story was all about time being marked, even to the point of *time* being the first thing created. However, in this story, we see nothing of time being mentioned. Again, tradition rears its head and tries to say otherwise. They use Genesis 2:4 and 3:8 for their justification of timing. Below is the King James Version using a translation that shows time. The New English Translation describes the action in its more literal sense with no real time stamp.

- "These are the generations of the heavens and of the earth when they were created, *in the day* that the LORD God made the earth and the heavens" (2:4, KJV).

- "This is the account of the heavens and the earth *when they were created*—when the LORD God made the earth and heavens" (2:4, NET).

- "And they heard the voice of the LORD God walking in the garden *in the cool of the day*" (3:8, KJV).

- "Then the man and his wife heard the sound of the LORD God moving about in the orchard *at the breezy time of the day*" (3:8, NET).

The second part of 2:4 has been assumed to be part of the second creation story. Anyone who reads English, or even Hebrew, understands this is, in reality, consistent with the first part of the sentence and will comprehend it is referring to the first creation story. Theologians are the culprits here since this is the only proper way to harmonize the two stories. I am so sorry, but this thesis does not pass any genuine sniff test.

Genesis 3:8 speaks about when the god visits Adam and Eve. Here is the spicy part! Here is the only part of the story that mentions a time-related occurrence: "The breezy time of day" is when the heat of the day does its thing—weather people call this convection. Depending on the area of the world, this can occur at any time of the day. There is one place I know for certain that does not experience this phenomenon, and that is Barstow, California. For the wind never stops blowing. Never, ever stops. Never. Ever.

This statement in the King James version is taken to mean the evening, as the sun is setting. This helps the notion that this stuff is done in one day. Okay, sure, but that is really limiting in the concept. The more I researched, the less I was able to accept this concept. Here again, I see tradition being taken as reality. We "know" for a fact that the wind only rises and blows in the late afternoon. Stupid meteorologists, thinking that something logical and normal occurs any time of the day. Pshaw!

The god of the second creation story has several attributes associated with his name (Yahweh Elohim). One of the most common is storm god. Marduk, Ba'al, El, and others have that title. Play along with me here; storms bring wind—a lot of wind if he is upset for any reason. If he is feeling mellow and wanting to, say, hang around and talk with his creation, the wind that occurs is gentler. Follow me in this. A literal transliteration of the Hebrew says, "And they are hearing the sound of Yahweh Elohim walking in the garden to (the) wind of the day."

When is the wind happening? There is no determinate to tell us when in the day. This says the storm god is walking through the garden and the sound of his steps was via the wind in the trees. Spend time in a pine forest, listen to the wind blow through the trees, and you can hear something, someone tromping through. This is the reason for this passage. A mighty god does not walk quietly, for it is not in his nature. Why is this so hard to understand?

Time is not important to the story, nor is there any attempt inside the story to merge this story with the first. What matters is the *why* of creating humanity. The why is for communion with the god. Adam knew of his god walking through the garden, knew full well of his god wanting to spend time with his creation. After all, this is the prime reason for all the cosmogony in this story.

Cosmology and Cosmogony

How nice if there were a word or two that helped us explain the difference between Baruch and Ezra. Two words that define each concept in the writing direction. Baruch ben Neriah wrote this second creation story intending to focus on humanity's origin stories. He did not do this in a way that is preached from any pulpit today. In this creation account, Baruch will use one of two theories of creation: cosmology and cosmogony. Both are rather similar since they both concern themselves with creation. Cosmology is *how* the universe came into being and *how* it became ordered. Cosmogony concerns itself with the *why* of creation. As we go through this process, we will see his determination of how these two theories are important.

The first creation story, written by Ezra after the exile, is about cosmology. An ordered and logical origin story that defined with such elegance what happened—and in an ordered way. The Cosmic Creator God, who was outside creation, caused our cosmos to be. As stated before, Ezra was committing to paper the Hebrew version of what and *how it happened.* The Cosmic Creator God, with a sure and steady hand, made things in a benign and careful way. At each step of the process, the god was pleased with the handiwork.

With our second creation story, Baruch was eager to present the why of creation, and so presented the second story, which *told of the reason* for Yahweh Elohim's purpose in doing the work. The god wished communion with humanity. We read of his careful attending to humanity's needs and even to spending time with them. This is what the theological commentaries and preaching have focused on for ages. That is, pardon the term, the preachable stuff.

Our author wanted his audience to see and get the flavor of cosmogony by having humanity take center stage. He filled the story with lush concepts that add so much to the storyline. Imagine a play that has no set or lighting. Actors worth their salt will still draw the audience in, but with a well-appointed set, the audience gets so much more, for they are able to process the intent better. Baruch does this. The stage and set are what he describes as the garden, both inside and outside.

Cosmology and cosmogony concepts are used throughout the story, sometimes changing places in the middle of a sentence or thought! The first creation story is built on a grand (cosmic) scale. In the second chapter, we observe intimacy, defined even to the point where we see the god being a personal god. The first hint to us is the name for the god that is used. In our first story, the name used is Elohim, which, as defined, is a description. That is why I often use the term Cosmic Creator God as a description in its place.

Baruch uses Elohim—Yahweh Elohim. This is his personal name, much like "Bond, James Bond." Here we get the first hint of the god who is personally interested in the welfare of humanity. He gets his hands dirty in the creation process of the first two humans. His care in performing the action is wildly different than the god in the first creation story. That god was the Cosmic Creator God, who is imagined as being rather separated from the origins that unfolded. The voicing used was similar commands to all creations: fish, land and animals, birds, and finally to humans. Two different facets of a singular god. The how and the why are presented starkly in these stories, as they are intended.

In the days of both Baruch and Ezra, naming something was not only special but necessary for understanding hierarchy. Yahweh named Adam, announcing his supremacy over humanity. Yahweh gave Adam power over all the creatures by making it his task to name them. Adam, in his delight, described Eve as his partner, and with that description we gain her name. God made Eve (Isha) to be an equal for Adam (Ish).

> And the Adam said, "This is now bone of my bone, and flesh of my flesh; she shall be called Isha, because she was taken out of Ish." —Genesis 2:23 (OJB)

Notice in the verse above the wording of Adam—"the Adam" (Ish). In the Hebrew, Adam was Ish until Isha came into the picture. I like the references to the Hebrew names for our human heroes in this story. Understanding the meaning of the names given in Hebrew will add a whole new level to what is transpiring. Adam was made from dirt and became living by the god breathing into his mouth. Eve was created by the god taking something from Adam. Their proper names in Hebrew are *Adamah* and *Chavah*.

Adam's name means "dirt," which is interesting since the breath of the god made him a living being. Eve was created from Dirt's body. Yet Eve's name (Chavah) is translated as "to breathe" or, more correctly, "to give life." Think of the later part of the story when, as the Christians tell it, the god "curses" Adam and Eve. He speaks about Adam's future dealing with dirt in order to live. Eve is told her giving life is going to be a problem from that time forward. If read attentively, the god does not curse Adam, nor does he curse Eve. What happens is Yahweh Elohim outlines what their lives will look like from then on. Adam will not have an easy time doing his gardening, plus caring for and protecting Eve and their kids at the same time. Eve will struggle with childbirth and need to rely on Adam for protection and sustenance.

Here is a slight paraphrase describing the future for Adamah (Dirt) and Chavah (To Breathe).

Dirt will deal with dirt

Until Dirt becomes dirt again;

To Breathe will suffer

To cause others to breathe;

Until To Breathe finally

Is unable to breathe anymore.

This is cosmogony. The insight here is nothing about curses, but an origin story telling the reader the reality of why humankind struggles to live and why they do not live forever. From the beginning, we gain insight into why life is a struggle. Two people are necessary for sustaining a workable life. And in the end, we are granted a ceasing of breath and a return to the earth.

From this, Jews from that time till now are pronounced dead when breath is not found, and burial is the only option.

The word *humanity* needs consideration here. Humanity is centered around man and woman as understood since the dawn of time. To fully understand the import of Yahweh Elohim's master plan, humanity needs to be replaced with the words *man* and *woman*.

> (Adam) said, "This is now bone of my bones, and flesh of my flesh; she shall be called Woman (Isha), Because she was taken out of Man (Ish)." For this reason a man (Ish) shall leave his father and his mother, and be joined to his wife (Isha); and they shall become one flesh. —Genesis 2:23–24 (AMP)

In the Hebrew, prior to woman being created from a part of man, Adam (Ish) is a neutral or androgynous term. Ish is human, but not a man or a male, because there was nothing to compare Ish to! When the god takes a part of Adam and makes Eve, the true nature of humanity is formed for both. Ish has the probability of becoming Adam, the human. Isha is on her way to becoming Eve. The only thing missing is a little Barry White.

Here is the logic structure: Ish cannot be Ish until Isha has been separated from Ish. The text specifically says that one cannot be fully human until there are two. One defines the other. From those two, they become one. This is so important later, as we shall see. Let us consider another view that reinforces this idea. *Eve* is not the pronoun used in the Hebrew texts. There we find the word *chavah*. This name is very important in its meaning for two distinct reasons. First, the meaning is "mother (protector) of all life." Also, when Chavah, the protector of life, gives birth to another life, there is joy. As we know, even to this day, a new birth brings joy to all. Second, Hebrews define much from the numerical values of words and letters. According to Rashi, the Medieval Jewish commentator, we find a completeness that is lost in translation and tradition. The woman with God will equal a man. More to the point, two equal halves make a whole. Let us do the math to see why this is important.

Chavah (הַוָה): (Cheth = 8, Va = 6, Hei = 5) Total value = 19

YHWH (הוהי): (Yod =10, He = 5, Waw = 6, He = 5) Total value = 26

19 + 26 = 45

Adam (אָדָם): (Aleph = 1, Daleth = 4, Mem = 40) Total value = 45

$$45 = 45$$

Cosmogony, dear reader, pure and simple.

So where do these items fit into ancient oral traditions? The garden, that place where Baruch placed his origin saga, is a compilation of incredibly old origin stories. We are told by people smarter than us it is easy to understand—yet we do not comprehend, let alone understand. We must be careful to put aside our twenty-first-century thinking when considering this most ancient of tales. It comes from so far in the past—the hoary, ancient, mist-filled past. I would not be surprised if Glog knew these stories when he conked Shug on her head and dragged her home to cook brontosaurus burgers for him. Yes, I know humans and dinosaurs did not exist together.[3] I am painting a picture showing how old these myths are.

Archaeology and anthropology tell us that ancient humans, in the earliest of times, were far down on the food chain. For eons, humanity was food for those on the predator list. With their limited defenses, they only kept a small area safe for the clan or tribe. These groups of people numbered fewer than fifty. That meant a definite delineation of labor was in place. The males kept watch, hunted, and fought off predators, both human and nonhuman. The females worked inside the boundary of safety, tending the fires and managing the calories needed for life. Children, pregnant mothers, and the old were tended by the women. I realize this is, by today's standards, misogynist. However, anthropologists, archaeologists, and sociologists agree this was a successful arrangement for the ancient peoples.

Men handled the very hazardous job of hunting and guarding those inside the safety zone. Women did everything else. Each received a benefit from this arrangement. The Garden of Eden was based on this arrangement. Adam worked and kept watch while Eve did the home things. And for you brighter readers, I am saying outright there was begetting going on in the garden. If we look deeper into the structure of the term *Garden of Eden*, we find its roots date back deep into the Akkadian language and that it

---

3   Sorry, not sorry, literalists. Dinosaurs and any form of humanity are separated by millions and millions of years.

means "a place that is well watered throughout." This has significance to our understanding. The entire region, from Mesopotamia through the Levant clear down to Egypt is a desert. Water is essential to life. Having a garden that is Eden is the primordial ideal for a living location. Outside the garden is the desert, a dry, harsh environment that will kill anyone naïve enough to wander out into it. And do not forget the snakes. With analogies, our story describes in simple terms the life that once was. We also gain understanding into the mindset of how the god, concerned for his greatest creation, worked to offer succor and love to those people.

Horrible Futures for All

According to our theologians, curses were flying everywhere fast and thick in this second creation story, and we of today even got caught in the crossfire. However, if one reads what is inside these curses, one finds they were not actual curses. When it comes to the cursing, the god saves the curses for the snake. The snake is not the devil, despite what evangelical preachers say. Genesis 3:1 says, "Now the serpent was more subtle than any other wild creature that the LORD God had made." A cat will knock something off a ledge, or a dog will eat your shoes. Cats and dogs do cat and dog things because that is what cats and dogs do. So, too, a snake—for they are subtle and sneaky. Here we have a magical snake, for it talks. I do not know of any snakes like that anymore. That kills my argument here about cats and dogs and snakes. Oh well.

Did the curse of the god make the snake's life any different from what it was before? It must have, according to tradition and extracurricular additions to the tale. Dear reader, snakes and people have, since the real dawn of time, held an animosity toward one another. From time immemorial, whether our ancestors were in the trees of the forest or jungle or out on the savannahs, the reality is that snakes sneak up on their prey. That is what a snake does, in a sneaky (snakey?) way. Perhaps this was a cosmogonical reason for the enmity between snakes and humanity? Consider, also, if snakes were to be so completely cursed, why did Moses' staff become a snake to convince the evil Egyptian king to let the Hebrew slaves go? Unfortunately for Moses and his snakey staff, the evil Egyptian king was not impressed with that act of magic, so God and Moses had to up their game with better magic.

After the people escaped and were tramping about in the desert, Moses was also commanded to make a bronze snake on a pole. If the people of Israel looked at it, they were healed. From snake bites. That the god had sent to punish the Israelites for grumbling about the bread they were given every day to eat. No, snakes were not anathema to those peoples from long ago; rather, snakes were feared and respected. And it was not only the Israelite people who thought this way. Myths from everywhere in the world acknowledge this human/snake interaction.

Adam was told in rather harsh terms that what he was doing in the garden would get much harder for the rest of his life.

The ground is cursed because of you; in painful toil you will eat of it all the days of your life.

Adam would have to fight for life with each breath and care for his family.

I will greatly multiply your pain in childbearing. In pain, you shall bring forth children and depend upon Adam to support the offspring.

Eve was to have greater difficulties during childbirth but, in her own way, would make the family stronger.

For what the snake got from its curse, we are unsympathetic. We are humans, and it is a snake. Christians love to insert all manner of future-telling into this story. Original sin, the devil, the devil's defeat by the Christ, the Yankees winning yet another World Series, and so on. None of these are present in the story—or even hinted at. These additions are a gloss, made up to give credence to that Jesus guy in the future. Remember, hindsight is 20/20. We get away with this embellishment because we are confident none of our ancestors will pop up tomorrow and castigate us for our "insights." By bending and twisting any story, one finds all manner of juicy items, if one looks hard enough.

> Now no shrub of the field had yet grown on the earth, and no plant of the field had yet sprouted, for the LORD God had not caused it to rain on the earth, and there was no man to cultivate the ground. —Genesis 2:5 (NET)

The god did something in his curse of Adam. Hidden in plain sight to us, the author's audience got the import. It passes us right over our heads today. What the first verse is saying is that there are no plants that are to be cultivated yet. This is referring to life-sustaining grains (oats, spelt, wheat, corn, barley). Since there are none of these plants in the garden, there is no need for rain. Grains and rain are not necessary because there is no one to do the hard work of cultivation.

> In painful toil you will eat of it all the days of your life. It will produce thorns and thistles for you, but you will eat the grain of the field. —Genesis 3:17–18 (NET)

Fast forward to the curse, and what do we find? Adam will have to do the hard, sweaty work of cultivation. He will be working the ground that will now have those grains available, and since those grains need rain to grow properly, the storm god will provide. But inside the words, the curse is present. With the rain comes the thorns and thistles will appear as well, for they need the rain to do their thing. These plants are cursed by every farmer across time and culture. Where life-giving grains grow, so will the cursed weeds. Cosmogony again! This origin story was ancient in oral form when, in the sixth century BCE, it was put on paper.

Final Thoughts

Take this story for what it is—multiple origin stories that were ingeniously sewn together. Humans, if they are lucky enough to survive birth and keep breathing, are due for one of two types of life: (1) the backbreaking work of laboring in the sun and dirt or (2) the exhausting work of childbirth. When the last breath is expelled, humans return to the dirt. Be sure to keep an eye out for the snake, the sneakiest predator. Genesis 2–3 is filled with why Yahweh Elohim created as he did. What happened inside the garden with his best creation is sad to us today because we insert morality and blame Adam and Eve for our woes. We are not bad because of what those two did— rather, we are assured that they are just like us. And that the god, personal god or storm god, cares for us and tends to our needs.

CHAPTER 6

Noah's Aquatic Adventures

Words change meaning over the course of their lives. Currently, the word *decimate* is changing from its original meaning of "reducing your own forces by one tenth" to "near extermination of a counterforce." Many other words have gone through this process. *Myth* and an associated term *mythos* have been subjected to this process. Mythos, in its original or technical sense, is "a traditional story of historical events that serves to unfold part of the world view of a people or explain a practice, belief, or natural phenomenon." When the term *myth* is used today, the understanding is "an unfounded or false notion." No, Walt Disney did not draw Mickey Mouse. The Declaration of Independence was not signed on July 4. Edison did not invent the lightbulb—and so on.

This is counter to what mythos/myth is. The first description is the true and accurate explanation for what is witnessed in the Hebrew testament. At its foundation, a myth is an attempt to explain something, an actual event that transpired sometime in the past. There is a kernel of truth that hides in plain sight in the stories. Genesis 1–11 is filled with mythos. In this book, they are called origin stories, for they explain why things are the way they are—and how the ancients explained how they came to be. In the myth of Noah and the flood, we find a truth that is ignored or obfuscated to the point that we cannot recognize what is being remembered. What occurred—the truth—is a catastrophic flood of mind-bending proportions that happened sometime in the past. What follows is an attempt to explain that flood and why it occurred.

The Background

As usual, we begin with an examination of who authored the passage and when it was penned. In the next chapter, we will examine closely when this natural occurrence happened—if it happened. This gives us a start to the timeline. Over the ages, this story was remembered and told in oral fashion, changing as needed to fit the peoples and regions where the survivors lived. As time passed, the story became stories, each transmitting different aspects of the occurrence. That is the nature of oral tradition. Sometime in the seventh century BCE, what was put to paper was a compilation of the various myths surrounding the flood. Again, I point to Baruch ben Neriah as the original compiler.

In this compilation, I do not see his style or personality. He is adept enough to use what is known, to weave the stories into a compact and dynamic whole. In what is written, even in translation, one feels the touch of how old these stories are. Included in the preamble are stories of giants and sons of God and heroes of old. For this compiler, these references are important, but to us of our age, they are incoherent and confusing. All that can be assessed about this is that it gives a reason for the actions of the god getting upset enough to cause the catastrophe.

Sometime in the exile, or just after, we see a redactor put his two cents' worth in—poorly, numerous times. How many clean animals did Noah take on the ark? How long did the flood waters take to subside? Which birds, and in what order, did Noah let loose? Why is Noah's age so important? All these questions arise because they have conflicting answers right inside the story or inserted in nonsensical ways. Why would they be added? It is not obvious unless the redactor wants to let his audience know something the compiler did not know. Stepping back and considering what is added allows the reader to understand who and why the additions are inserted. Ezra is the redactor, and his insertions are to add weight to the new form of belief system that he is pushing.

In encapsulated form, here is the story: humanity was behaving very, very badly. Sons of god were making whoopie (and babies) with the daughters of men. Giants were roaming the land. People were not being nice to one another. And the Yankees were winning yet another World Series. The Cosmic Creator God, after talking to himself, chose to end his experiment but would keep one human and his family to start over. God told Noah to build a boat, fill it with animals, and ride the storm out. He flooded the earth, saving only his special human and family, and hoped for a better outcome. Noah did his thing, the god did his thing, and the process started all over again. The end.

From an Early Age

My troubles with this saga began early. Various questions kept interrupting me from the official storyline. I did not understand the disconnect between what I was told from the pulpit and in Sunday school from what I read. My recollection of Sunday school had cutesy pictures of animals lining up two-by-two to enter the ark, with Noah looking on rather benignly. Closing my eyes, I still see the pictures of Noah and giraffes looking out the window as the ark floats cheerfully on the top of cute waves. "It rained and poured for forty long days-ies days-ies, Almost drove those animals crazy craz-ies, children of the Lord," we sang to a delightfully catchy tune. What fun! But my mind never went there. Rather, I was saddened, for the death of the entire world was, to my young mind, a violent and harsh catastrophe. It was not right to portray the story as fun and happy, like a day at Disneyland. Every soul, every animal, every spider, and bird, every lion and tiger and bear (oh, my!) was destroyed by the anger of the Cosmic Creator God. I was left sleepless on multiple occasions, mulling over the horror I felt.

I know what the story told about the sin, noise, monster sex, and other problems that angered the Cosmic Creator God. To my mind then, and even now, this god reminded me of a young child who destroyed his building blocks in a fit of anger because of an infantile issue of the moment. How could this be true? What was the problem with the animals? How were they to blame? Were the birds secretly Dallas Cowboys fans? And humanity—

were they, each and every single one—evil? Abraham went toe-to-toe with his god over Sodom. How was this different? Noah was the only one who found favor with the god in Genesis 6. Only one person out of all the people? We know from the after-report of the flood that one of his kids was still of the old order of bad. The underlying reason for such a natural catastrophe is told in this ages-old myth, but it continued to puzzle and frighten me.

Questions Asked

To gain insight into understanding these questions, several more questions need to be asked, and answers must be found. First, however, articles of belief need to be shed. Theological mumbo-jumbo has to go. Tradition is next. These biases are deeply rooted in one's mind and must be excised in order to know what must be asked. "Clear the mechanism," is what is needed.[1] Focus on what is in front of us and see it clearly. Let us get some questions and see what direction we will go in answering these.

- Did a flood of epic proportions occur?
- When did the flood happen?
- *Is this a unique story?* Are there other stories like this?
- How could the flood be so big?
- Was the flood worldwide?

I have been told by my betters that every society across the world, as we know it today, has flood stories that are akin to the Noah story.[2] That is all well and good, but the real question is not *did* a cataclysmic flood occur in the region, but *when*? The Cosmic Creator God, when he does things, does them logically and with ordinary things lying about his house. *When* the flood happened is vital to give relevance to our quest, for it must make sense to our story as well as help describe what happened. Is there a time in history that includes the ingredients for a flood of such proportions? Yes, there is a logical time frame when this saga occurred. We will discuss

---

1   "Clear the mechanism" is a term used by Kevin Costner in the movie *For Love of the Game*. It refers to silencing the outside noise and focusing solely on what is at hand.

2   This is patently not true. For example, Africa has no flood stories. Pacific Islanders' recollections are of tsunami-type flooding.

this further later on. We need to turn to traditional dating to see if there is a logical time frame.

Archbishop James Ussher gets first crack. His mathematical genius and incorruptible calculator say the flood occurred in 2348 BCE, just before the six o'clock news. With a bit of research, this date is silly and is to be laughed at. The Great Pyramid of Cheops was finished in 2560. Egyptian records show no flood—other than the normal thing the Nile does every year. Civilizations all through Anatolia and south to the bottom of Mesopotamia were flourishing and had no pause until the twelfth century BCE. Therefore, this time frame is out.

After a thorough check of asteroids, meteor impacts, volcanic eruptions, or earthquakes reported via oral culture or archaeological finds, nothing happened for thousands of years around our region of inquiry. None were recorded. Other parts of the world sustained one or many of those catastrophes throughout history but do not affect our geography. We see tidal waves of epic proportions throughout coastal regions, both now and through history. Regions in the northern hemisphere had similar issues as are being considered in this chapter. But they were not part of the world as was known in the region we are discussing, and so they are not important.

When would the environment have been right for our needs? One must look further into the past than the twenty-fourth century BCE. Eleven thousand years ago, at the end of the Pleistocene period, when the last ice age was ending, is where we land.[3] A perfect storm was brewing, one might say. As the ice sheets melted, the oceans rose. Coastlines were inundated. Rainfall and ice dams failing brought never-before-seen flooding beyond belief.[4] Downstream, those floods devastated the land and swept all living things away. Archaeology has proven such devastation over and over. These actions are, without a doubt, the origin of these myth stories. Across the world, in areas close to the evaporating ice that once held our world in its arms, we find stories and evidence for those stories. This era is known as the Holocene

---

3   This will be discussed further in a later chapter.

4   Lake Agassiz's creation of the Great Lakes and the Mississippi River plus Lake Missoula causing the Scablands and influencing the Columbia River Gorge are but two examples.

period. We are still in that period. Circa eighty centuries ago, the event that started the process for our story happened. That event was the opening of what is now known as the Bosphorus Strait emptying into the Black Sea. And off to the races we go!

Other Flood Myths

When considering the Noah story, we have another myth that must be considered that helps us gain insight into our Genesis account. I am referring to the Akkadian myth, the *Epic of Gilgamesh*. The oldest extant writing we have is from Sumer, sometime between 2750 and 2500 BCE. Here we find our Mesopotamian Noah, who is named either Utna'pishtim or Atra'hasis. The name change depends on which city-state the writing is from. The oldest known story has the hero named Ziusudra, the last king of the Sumerian city-state Shuruppak. He is the last preflood king mentioned in the Sumerian King List. The name *Ziusudra* is Sumerian and is translated into Akkadian as Utna'pishtim. We are interested in tablets eleven and twelve of the *Epic of Gilgamesh*. The hero, Gilgamesh, distraught by his friend Enkidu's death, has undertaken a perilous journey to find immortality. He seeks and finds Utna'pishtim and his wife, since they gained freedom from death. They became immortal because they obeyed the order of a god to build a round boat in a week, put some animals in it, and weather the approaching storm. The story arc (in tablets eleven and twelve) is amazingly similar to the Genesis flood. This myth's earliest writings are millennia older than what we find in Genesis. Finding this myth and all its interesting redactions is confirmation that something happened in the Ancient Near East (ANE). It is a *Flood. Of. Epic. Proportions.* Theological detractors claim, by manipulating the dating, that the Mesopotamian stories were copied from the Hebrew story. This is false—archeology shows otherwise. Another argument revolves around Noah's story being written by Moses, so it must be true.

Preachers insist those other, older Mesopotamian stories are made up and not to be considered. Try and, if possible, follow their logic: "Of course these two myths are similar, but they are not the same. If they are not exactly the same, one must be false. Therefore, one must be lying, and it cannot be the Hebrew story." This is a silly argument to have and is being kept alive from ego alone. This logic tree is shaky and lacks solid roots. The logic of this is that the Hebrew writings must stand alone, with no outside influence. What matters is, again, something happened—and what is our takeaway to be? A corroboration is needed for our Noah story and, as seen, is found in Mesopotamian sources. A bit of reasoning will show insight into why these stories are from the same fundamental source, and why that matters.

Some readers may still be wondering how or why the Hebrew story aligns with the Mesopotamian story, although with differences. First, there is no tangible way a flood could happen in Canaan as described. Why would this saga spring forth from the hoary past into the Hebrew mythology if there is no foundational reason for its existence? Excellent question. And there is a beautiful answer that is most certainly not taught from the pulpit. I argue this story came from Abraham's childhood in Ur, for that city-state is part of the southern Mesopotamia flood plain, right in the way of the supposed flood's path. If we consider more broadly (and farther back into time), the Canaanites, as well as others on the Mesopotamian seaboard, are related to the Akkadians and other Mesopotamians who lived farther to the north—those people whose ancestors were affected by the flood.

A perplexing problem that has withstood typical thinking is to understand how both watercraft (Noah's and Utna'pishtim's) were finally deposited on various mountains in northern Anatolia—upstream from where they supposedly started by hundreds of miles. After thousands and thousands of years and migrations of hundreds of miles, the story changed to suit the environment of where they were. The myth is true; the names and locations were changed to suit the people of the times and locations. A life-altering event such as the flood will travel well through the ages, through the geography, and through the dispersion of people. All of that is possible. But we have a logistical problem that needs to be mentioned.

As stated above, Canaan is out for a flood, but Mesopotamian flood plains are a good possibility. The most probable place for this flood is far to the north, in the Caucus Mountains, along the southeast shores of the Black Sea. If we take the two traditional spots for the flood occurring, how do nonpowered, unsteerable boats move against the water's movement in that part of the world? Utna'pishtim and Noah's boats went north, against the drainage of waters. Such a thing will not happen. The reason they landed where they did, in the mountains far to the north, is because this is where they started. Mount Sapon and Mount Ararat (if that is really where it landed) are considered sacred mountains, secured for the gods' personal residence (temple). Myths from Ugarit, Mesopotamia, Canaan, and Scythia all attest to these Caucus regions for such temples.

The Noah story depicts a boat that is a rectangular box. The Utna'pishtim saga depicts a large, circular craft. Both are hideously large, and neither design was in the capability of ship-makers of that time—or for ages to come. The circular boat, we are told, is silly and impractical. Who in their right mind conjured such a convoluted watercraft? Our take today tells us Noah's ark looks like the one at the Creation Museum in Kentucky. Alas, Noah's ark was, instead, a rectangular box without a swept front and back as we normally see on watercraft. A rectangular box is even worse than a circular boat for weathering large bodies of water. However, the round type of boat has been used on the Tigris and Euphrates rivers for eons. Coracles, as they are known in England, are still used there as personal watercraft. Where would the original story, that hoary eons of old myth, have likely been generated from? Is it a round boat or a rectangular box? Flooding of such proportions can also be understood in Mesopotamia simply by looking at the land, which is a flood plain that is sourced from two major rivers that originate in the far north. An assumption is made in the literalists' viewpoint that the Noah story occurred in Canaan. Again, by looking at the geography, we must agree this is not a place that is a candidate for a flood.

According to both stories, the flood was worldwide. A definition of what constituted the world at that time is required. Today, we think of the world as that blue marble hanging in space. Is this what the people of that time understood? We find that information after the flood in what is termed *the Table of Nations* in Genesis 10. In this part of the text, we read the genealogy of the three sons of Noah: Ham, Shem, and Japeth. They are more about geography than population groups, which approximates the division of the world as it was known then. I see no China, no Scandinavian countries, no Australia or the Americas—these are as unknown as the dinosaurs. England, Iceland, and the Antarctic have no place in the knowledge base of the time. India and anything south of the headwaters of the Nile are not referenced. The Ancient Near East's knowledge of the world was limited compared to our world today. We need to remember that in their time, travel from one end of their world to another takes a year or more. With that in mind, it is not impossible to believe their world as they knew it was fearfully large.

Here are the limits as defined in the Table of Nations:

- **East:** To southwest Iran (Elam)
- **West:** To southern Spain (Tarshish)
- **South:** To East Africa (Seba) and Yemen (Sheba)
- **North:** To Ukraine (Ashkenaz, the Scythians)

Today's Mindset

If twenty-first-century people ever wanted to see the reality of how the ancients viewed life, this is the penultimate example. Here we get a real-life reality check of how our ancestors lived and thought. To use an old adage, gods and humanity were opposite sides of a coin. What mattered to them was not which side was in focus, but the coin itself—that's what reality revolved around. The ancients did not and could not remove one side's actions from the other. The flood survivors saw total devastation in every part of their existence. There must have been something equally wrong to have caused such anger from the god. What was so great a sin that the god would have destroyed the world? For the ancients, this was an easy decision. The whole of humanity had to be at fault. What else could the answer be? Total human depravity + a god's wrath = worldwide destruction.

Imagine some scenarios from our lives today that can bring this thought process closer to home.

- You arrive at work, and everyone tells you the boss wants to see you immediately.

- Your spouse tells you, "We need to talk."

- The school calls and says the principal needs to see you regarding one of your children.

- You are using your credit card, and it is declined.

What is your first, immediate response? For each of us, at that moment, the answer is, *"What is wrong?"* Our heartbeat rises, our mind goes blank, our hands get clammy, and our eyes look frantically about for an escape. This is the very normal way a human reacts to inputs such as these examples. If you did not answer that way, you are not being truthful. Humanity, since even before the flood, is hard-wired to think this way. The flood story is the best example showing that part of life: a problem arises, and our response is, "What did I do wrong?" For the ancients, the immediate response was, "What did I do to anger the gods?" Read the math above, for it gives the import of why this destruction occurred. Here, in the preamble to the flood story, the reason for the destruction to come is stated. Most of this is gibberish to us, but in the compiler's day, all this made sense. Upon careful reading, the god is not upset at the giants or the sons of God, but his focus is on the human race and its wickedness. Tradition spends a bit of time on humanity but loves to go on about those other two categories!

> When human beings began to increase in number on the earth and daughters were born to them, the sons of God saw that the daughters of humans were beautiful, and they married any of them they chose. Then the LORD said, "My Spirit will not contend with humans forever, for they are mortal. Their days will be a hundred and twenty years." The Nephilim were on the earth in those days—and also afterward—when the sons of God went to the daughters of humans and had children with them. They were the heroes of old, men of renown.

> The LORD saw how great the wickedness of the human race had become on the earth, and that every inclination of the thoughts of the human heart was only evil all the time. The LORD regretted that he had made human beings on the earth, and his heart was deeply troubled. So the LORD said, "I will wipe from the face of the earth the human race I have created—and with them the animals, the birds and the creatures that move along the ground—for I regret that I have made them." But Noah found favor in the eyes of the LORD. —Genesis 6:1–8 (NIV)

In Mesopotamian mythology, Enlil is tired of the noise humans made. He sends a drought to kill them off, and then a pestilence, and finally a famine. None of these attacks does the job because the humans cried out to the god Enki, who helps them weather the attacks. Enlil goes postal and, with the help of other gods, sends a flood, which will do the job. Using a bit of subterfuge, Enki tells Atra'hasis (Utna'pishtim) of the coming apocalypse. An ark and some animals later, humanity and animals are saved. Upon learning of Enki helping humanity, there are reprisals, strongly worded letters, and vicious backstabbing.

Discussed briefly above is the associated background of both the Hebrew people and Mesopotamia. The term to be considered is *Semite*. Arabs, Jews, Akkadians, Ugarit, and Phoenicians are all part of an original language group: the Semitic language peoples. About ten thousand years ago, they started migrating from the Caucus Mountain region south into Mesopotamia where they met southern tribes in cities like Ur. Others, traveling west, moved until they reached the Mediterranean Sea, where some turned south and entered and settled what is now Canaan. Suppose, just suppose, that our flood did not occur after the migration happened, but before. What is easier to see, a flood of epic proportions along a flood plain that ravaged that valley, or a cataclysmic rain event that flooded whole regions until natural dams and mountain passes were overcome?

Look back to the north, up in the Caucus Mountain region. Whole valleys filling with water, smaller peaks being submerged, and whole communities being washed away in the relentless rain and storm. Mountains crumbling and passages from one valley to another opening to devastate the other valleys yet again. Ten thousand years ago, these people were coming out of the ice age. Life ceased to exist under a year of torrential rain. Some people survived, and the event was welded into their psyches, for we know of this story today. And this makes complete sense, for all the pieces fit together so well. Noah or Utna'pishtim—it does not matter. A boat or raft of some sort was made, and they stuck every animal they could find on board. Humanity can be extremely resourceful when the need arises. Here is yet another example of that very instance.

Finally, Some Answers

With the facts in hand, let us put things together and get a clearer, nonmetaphysical understanding of this story. Fortunately, with the data presented above, we can confidently answer questions for both the Hebrew and Mesopotamian stories and why this story has been kept alive for seven thousand years.

- *Was there a flood?* Yes, without a doubt.

- *Was all of humanity and animal life lost, except for a handful of people?* Yes—most certainly, in that area.

- *Did the god do it because he was angry with humanity?* According to their understanding, of course the god was angry, and yes, he did.

- *Did the god regret his actions?* Yes, and the Hebrew story included a reminder (the rainbow) for himself to never do it again.

- *Was there a Noah or Utna'pishtim (or another of his aliases)?* There was some quick-witted person who was able to spring into action and save his family.

- *What about the animals carried on the ark?* I often read about people saving animals during moments of catastrophe, so yes.

Does this mean that we call shenanigans in the story and regard it as a highly embellished lie? Absolutely not! Something happened. A flood of epic proportions occurred in the past. When and where and what caused it can be argued until Jesus returns. The whole of this story is about the ancients working to account for the *why*. Do not look down on these people, for although they did not have science to explain things, they were not stupid, nor unable to reason. Most certainly, this is a group of origin stories, ancient oral traditions lasting throughout the ages. We have gained insight into explaining why a catastrophic flood would imperil the known world: rampant and overreaching sin. We know why rainbows are present after a storm; it is the promise of the god. Being true to a god allows one to become not only a survivor but also earn greatness from honoring your god.

CHAPTER 7

A Godly Kick in the Pants

The Tower of Babel is a favorite story that describes humanity reaching toward heaven to make themselves equal to their god. Such pride, such ambition, such disobedience is shown that the Cosmic Creator God has to put humanity in its place by disrupting their speech, which forces them to scatter across the face of the earth.

> The whole earth had a common language and a common vocabulary. When the people moved eastward, they found a plain in Shinar and settled there. Then they said to one another, "Come, let's make bricks and bake them thoroughly." (They had brick instead of stone and tar instead of mortar.) Then they said, "Come, let's build ourselves a city and a tower with its top in the heavens so that we may make a name for ourselves. Otherwise, we will be scattered across the face of the entire earth." —Genesis 11:1–4 (NET)

Theology is off to the races regarding this epic story with the following arguments: humanity thought they could reach heaven by their own actions. They used the stuff they themselves were made of (dirt), instead of god-made materials (stone). Humanity built the tower to glorify themselves instead of glorifying their god. Unity of humanity, we are told, is used both for the noble and the ignoble. This unity was bad, for it showed hubris and a disdain for the god. Such rebellion and pride caused the god to intervene and stop such sinfulness. The Christian Trinity is seen here, for the god says, "Come, let us go down." Who else could he be speaking to other than Jesus and the Holy Spirit? Fundamental evangelicals see the same sinfulness today at the particle accelerator CERN, for scientists seek to unlock the "god particle," the fundamental mystery of life. That sums up the sermonizing well. I am sure some items have slipped through the cracks, but this is a fine representation of what has been theologically discovered in these few verses.

> But the LORD came down to see the city and the tower that the people had started building. And the LORD said, "If as one people all sharing a common language they have begun to do this, then nothing they plan to do will be beyond them. Come, let's go down and confuse their language so they won't be able to understand each other." —Genesis 11:5–7 (NET)

We are to think that humanity is the Hulk smashing Loki and saying, "Puny god" as he walks away. Am I to believe, from what this thinking leads me to, is that the Cosmic Creator God is afraid of humanity when united in purpose? Or is there another possible way to see this story? Possibly, just possibly, a way of thought that shows a different side to humanity? Perhaps humanity is being human, not prideful, but with a dollop of PTSD? With this in mind, do we get to see the Cosmic Creator God acting as a kind and loving god? I know, crazy talk! Let's consider this angle and see where we get.

Origins

In this saga of Babel, we do not have compiler and redactor. The way the story is built, two people doing the work makes little sense. This event is predicated from the hoary past of Mesopotamia. With that in mind, the original stories are reworked into what we know at the time of the exile. So many of our primordial epochs in the first part of Genesis have origins that spring from the ancient history of that region, far to the east of Canaan. In our discussion, two myths are spun together to give us the storyline. In the epic of Enmerkar, the god Enki (yes, him again) is ascribed as the one who multiplied the languages of humanity. This is far different from what is told in our Babel story where Yahweh merely mixed up common speech (made it gibberish).

The physical tower is associated with King Nimrod, who directed a tower to be built "with its head in heaven." The Greek historian Herodotus puts the tower in Babylon and says that it was the tower of the god Marduk. E'temen'an'ki was known as the biblical tower until archaeology realized the proper tower was actually the god Nabu's temple in Borsippa. A close reading of our story shows us the use of the Hebrew word *migdal*, translating to "tower," "fortress," or "citadel." Our story says nothing about our tower having any religious connotation either, but hey, tradition! With these two items, the mixing of languages and a handy tower, we now can put the claim to the test. A Hebrew writer in Babylon during the exile heard of these two stories and realized there was worth in mixing these two Mesopotamian events into a powerful origin story for the Hebrew people. What he did was compile the myths together into a coherent whole—then added some commentary to aid his listeners in following the story. Further below, we divide the story into two parts: the original and the commentary. His masterful work has been so insightful, we know of it today.

Sometime after the flood occurred, way to the north in the Black Sea region, the survivors and their families as a whole migrated to the east. Which was really south. Upon arriving in the Mesopotamian river valley at a place called Shinar, they stopped.[1] Pleased with what they saw, they built a city—a city with a wall and a high point. A tower, one might say. They were pleased with the plan. All of them huddled together, secure in the thought of "united we stand, divided we fall," "safety in numbers," "You go first, I'll watch," or something like that. Since they all spoke the same language, consensus was achieved quickly about staying together. The god saw what was happening, both in their words and deeds. He said to himself (himselves?), "We need to put a stop to this. Noah's kids need to leave the nest and go out on their own." The god then messed with words and speech. People did not understand each other, so they left for parts unknown.

Humanity was scared. That fear is best described as post-traumatic stress disorder (PTSD). Humanity had experienced what happened when stuff got wonky during the flood. Better to stay together, so all would know when someone did something really stupid. Rather than that stupidity getting out of hand and becoming endemic, the problem could be nipped in the bud. It was

---

1   Shinar is the region between Babylon and the Persian Gulf.

not the fear of the unknown but the fear of what had happened to the entire world. Fear brings a smallness of thought: shut down and build protective walls. We see this happening to those migrants. What we see here is fear and disregard for the promise of the blessing of the Cosmic Creator God to Noah and Adam. What was that directive, or blessing, humanity was ignoring?

> And God blessed them, and God said to them, "Be fruitful and multiply, and fill the earth and subdue it; and have dominion over the fish of the sea and over the birds of the air and over every living thing that moves upon the earth." —Genesis 1:28 (RSV)

> And God blessed Noah and his sons, and said unto them, "Be fruitful, and multiply, *and replenish the earth.*" —Genesis 9:1 (ASV)

A people full of fear could not see the future joys of a promise for them and for their future offspring.

> And they said, "Come, let us build us a city, and a tower, whose top may reach unto heaven, and let us make us a name; *lest we be scattered abroad upon the face of the whole earth.*" —Genesis 11:4 (ASV)

Parenting 101

Parents delight in seeing their children take on new and different challenges. Children will find obstacles in the beginning, struggle to learn the basics, and, for a time, fight against attempts to help them break through to the wonders of competence. Here is where parents flourish—steady, loving support with kind words. Yes, an occasional kick in the pants is necessary, but what the child needs is firm and strong support. A rock to lean against during the storm's worst. When they finally break free of those restraints, unlimited joy propels them further. The Cosmic Creator God is that very loving parent in this story. He sees the fear of the past. With love and a kick in the pants, he gets humanity back to living the promise he offered Adam and Noah. Replenish the whole earth! We even see humanity has lost the first part of the blessing via their words there in the city with the tower. No word is mentioned of being fruitful and multiplying. What impact fear has when it occludes even part of a bright future. Here, the fullness of a blessing has completely disappeared into the ether.

Much theology has been spent on trivia in this story; the tower looms largest for the small time it is mentioned in the Bible. The tower's location and the impact of that location are also in focus, as well as how word play is important (Babel and babble). Did the god confound, confuse, mangle, or pull a switch-a-roonie to their speech? Let us put these things to rest right now. In this particular setting of life, a tower and the city walls are integral to safety and security. A tower gives a commanding view of what is outside the walls. In those times, the tower is part of the wall complex. Building a tower that "reaches to the heavens" is good for the city's defense, as well as making a name for the city. Better walls and higher towers gave good street cred for those cities. Of course, such things as walls and towers meant it was harder to fight against. But that is relegated to the unimportant stack of stuff in Sunday school.

Fast forward to Medieval times. Multiple high towers were integral to the wall complex. Higher towers were often the residences of kings and their families, just as central towers were where the gods (and their earthly kings) lived in ancient times. In ancient times, better fortifications also meant your god was higher on the god food chain, which meant your city was too. Archaeologists believe the Tower of Babel is the ziggurat at Borsippa. We have reference to this tower made by Nebuchadnezzar, who rebuilt the ziggurat (tower) there. Borsippa, a small, backwater city without a rhyming name. The tower got "moved" to Babylon, where puns could be inserted. Hebrew wording, which has not come down to us literally, uses fun word play. Many words imply other words that allow meanings that indicate confusion and incoherence in the words and actions of humanity. Tradition says Yahweh's words and actions do not include word games like that, despite what we read. They are simple and concise. All this is to say, when the story was told, the hearers understood that people were confused—but their god was not. What fun we miss out on!

Technology Advances

What silly people, using baked (burned) bricks, instead of using stone. How cavemanlike! Our story here is often used as a reference for Jesus' parable of building a house on the sand. Surely they knew stone was better and more long-lived than hardened mud! Um, do you remember where these people were? They lived in between two rivers on a vast flood plain! A plain that is flatter than a squashed bug on a windshield, hundreds of miles from any location that had more than mud. Where, oh where, were these silly people supposed to get stone? Using bitumen for a binding agent was smart. It was as readily available as the mud they used. That stuff oozed out of the ground throughout Mesopotamia, but mostly at Hit, in the middle region of the river valley, in the land of Shinar.[2]

Bitumen is a thick, oozy oil that adheres well to baked bricks. It has waterproofing properties, and when straw is added, it makes a very tight bond to the brick—a good choice that suits the purposes, I think.[3] This is a high technological advancement. Here, too, we see another leap of humanity. This type of building technology allowed multi-story buildings as well as higher, stronger fortifications not found before this time, whenever that time was. Roadways and water conduits could be built. Separate locations of life-giving water and farming could be joined easily. Water could travel better and farther and could be directed, knowing the water course laid out will stay in its intended path. Crops could grow over a larger area and more evenly. Food industries we rarely think of started up and expanded. Date palms, vineyards, olive groves, and fruit and nut orchards were created. These industries came about from getting water to places far from the rivers. A myriad of jobs are created. Artisans flourished, making all manner of items from furniture to clothing. Fine articles of jewelry and artwork flooded the market. Trade between people in the city grew outward, seeking export as well as importing other wanted items.

Ovens hot enough to fire those bricks had to be invented. Creative uses of various types of clay allowed ceramics, pottery, and suchlike to arise and become commonplace. Exotic metals could be created and formed in those ovens. Brass, bronze, gold, and silver became items for everyday use, as well as trade and, yes, warfare. Ovens created more uses for bitumen. As a glue, it could repair broken pottery. Waterproofing enabled watercraft to be

---

2   Hit is just north of Ramadi, adjacent to the Euphrates River.

3   Bitumen and its byproducts are still being mined to this day in the region.

built stronger and lighter. Jewelry, musical instruments, and statuary have been found created out of this substance. Bitumen compounds were used as insecticides and disinfectants and even some medical remedies. Over in Egypt, bitumen was used for embalming.

Literary Styling

Here is the whole of the story. Highlighted is what is unnecessary to the intent of the story. People back in the day knew all of the extraneous stuff, but it made for a more interesting time both in the reading and listening to the story. Following is the story as found in Genesis. The underlined parts, the fluff (commentary), are what we have grown accustomed to hearing and thinking about. Our gold is passed over too often because of the commentary.

> Now the whole earth had one language and few words. And as men migrated from the east, they found a plain in the land of Shinar and settled there. And they said to one another, "Come, let us make bricks, and burn them thoroughly." And they had brick for stone, and bitumen for mortar. Then they said, "Come, let us build ourselves a city, and a tower with its top in the heavens, and let us make a name for ourselves, lest we be scattered abroad upon the face of the whole earth." And the LORD came down to see the city and the tower, which the sons of men had built. And the LORD said, "Behold, they are one people, and they have all one language; and this is only the beginning of what they will do; and nothing that they propose to do will now be impossible for them. Come, let us go down, and there confuse their language, that they may not understand one another's speech." So the LORD scattered them abroad from there over the face of all the earth, and they left off building the city. Therefore, its name was called Babel, because there the LORD confused the language of all the earth; and from there, the LORD scattered them abroad over the face of all the earth. —Genesis 11:1–9 (RSVCE)

Below is the rewrite of above, without the underlined words. We see a completely different take on the story. What we see is what the author desires his audience to get. In his day, his audience had no problem with what you are about to read.

> Now the whole earth had one language and few words. As men migrated from the east and settled, they said, "Lest we be scattered abroad upon the face of the whole earth." The Lord said, "Behold, they are one people,

and they have all one language; and this is only the beginning of what they will do; and nothing that they propose to do will now be impossible for them." "Come, confuse their language, that they may not understand one another's speech." So, the Lord scattered them abroad from there over the face of all the earth, and from there the Lord scattered them abroad over the face of all the earth.

Not unlike a parent whose child is afraid to do something that will bring great joy to them, the Cosmic Creator God sees his children, humanity, unable to partake of his blessing. *To be fruitful and multiply*, and *to subdue the whole world* is what he offered to both Noah and Adam. The god here in this story removes the two impediments to their reaching out and grabbing the brass ring of life.

I remember way back in time. My daughter wanted to learn how to jump off the diving board of our pool. She had her parent's encouragement as well as her brother's. Day after day, she stood at the edge of the board, afraid. She knew her fear was unfounded. She had seen her parents, brother, and friends dive or jump. We had all survived. Finally, as a dad is supposed to do, I told her, "Either get in the pool, or get off the board. If you don't jump, you are barred from the diving board for the rest of the year." She glared daggers at me—and jumped.[4] Imagine the surprise and delight on her face when she surfaced and swam to the ladder. She shrieked, "Wait, wait, I want to do it again!" Again and again, laughing as she ran to the board and jumped into the pool. Nevermore afraid.

A wonderful set of origin stories—how separate languages came into being and the reason for the dispersion of peoples in the Table of Nations. Yahweh is again shown to be a caring god who wants the best for his chosen people, and we see how all the nations (city-states and tribes) come from a common source.

Finally

The Cosmic Creator God did not judge the people of this account; there was no sin to punish. Pride was not in evidence; fear was the primary emotion.

---

4   Anyone who knows my daughter knows that glare and trembles before its power . . .

Forgotten was the option to jump and the promise of fun afterward. A parent wants the best for his children. The Cosmic Creator God wanted the same thing. Humanity, in this story, wanted to make a name for themselves by cowering behind a tower. By being kicked out of the house, the name they honed was bigger and much more powerful than they could have realized. Don't believe me? Why then are we talking about them millennia after they did what they did?

'Nuff said.

Brothers at Arms

CHAPTER 8

A Biblical Drive-By

Brothers are featured almost to the exclusion of other familial ties in Genesis. First onstage are Cain and Abel. We see Isaac and Ishmael next, followed by Jacob and Esau. The last brother story has ten brothers against one. The hero in the last act is Joseph. (He had a technicolor dream coat and looked a lot like Donny Osmond.) There is no end to the theological and moral issues regarding the brother/brother interactions, but this discussion will only consider Cain and Abel.

When I think about the story of Cain and Abel, I cannot help but hum the catchy tune from *Oklahoma!*, "The Farmer and the Cowman Should Be Friends." The song made the problem out to be light and simple. As the Broadway play unfolds, the actual issues turn out very sinister, with envy, hate, and hate's partner, death, stalking and waiting at every turn. Preachers get good mileage from the Very First Murder in the Bible as well as the Real Meaning behind the god turning his back on Cain's offering. We can talk all day about the enmity between farmers (sedentary) and cowmen (nomads), for this has been a problem throughout the ages. There is plenty to contemplate regarding how civilization gained the ability to coax life from the ground. The cowmen (nomads) did not need what the city offered, but city folk needed the nomads. Hey, a city guy has to eat, does he not?

Upon reflection, this has absolutely nothing to do with the story of Cain and Abel. What occurs in the story focuses upon the interaction of Cain and his god. The preamble of Cain, a farmer, and Abel, an animal caretaker, exists only to set up the important part of the offering-to-their-god schtick. What the author wants us to know is that (1) the Cosmic Creator God did not accept Cain's offering, and (2) Cain's response to that issue. Despite all the preaching that tells otherwise, no answer is given—nor hinted at—for why Cain's offering got ignored. It is the whim of the god; his reason is ineffable and frankly, none of your business. More important to our discussion is the interaction between humans in side-by-side living. Brothers, or siblings, to broaden it out a bit, are the most intimate of human life. Existence side-by-side requires cooperation side-by-side. This equation becomes far more important when civilization comes into being.

Understanding this story fully in its context is not what is found in Sunday school—rather, it is in the scheme that started in the Garden of Eden. There we find that Adam rebelled not so much against his god but, more to the point, against himself. What is found in the Cain and Abel story is that Cain rebelled against his brother. Seen another way, it was an act against his community. All humanity is a brother to every other human. Today, our community is worldwide. Everyone is related and for two simple reasons. We all carry the breath of Yahweh Elohim. We all carry the one thing inside that is the god's alone, our blood, for it is the life of each of us. To deprive anyone of us of those two parts, breath and blood, is to take the place of the god. His judgment of this is death by separation, as we saw in the garden and which will be seen here as well.

This story revolves around Cain, for he and his god are the only actors with lines in this play. Cain and Abel bring sacrifices to their god, who rejects Cain's offering for no apparent reason. Yahweh was pleased with Abel's sacrifice; we are told how cool and wonderful that sacrifice was.[1] Cain makes up a story about this rejection and causes himself distress. The story he made up is that the god rejected his offering and was pleased with Abel's gift, which, upon further reflection, meant the god must not like Cain. Cain

---

1   The manner in which Abel's sacrifice is spoken about and what parts are reserved for Yahweh's portion are indicative of our pre-exilist's writing.

becomes filled with envy. Despite what is preached, envy is not a sin, nor is it a moral issue. It causes upset, and the conversation between the god and Cain speaks to this very upset:

> Cain was very angry, and his countenance fell. The LORD said to Cain, "Why are you angry, and why has your countenance fallen? If you do well, will you not be accepted? And if you do not do well, sin is couching at the door;[2] its desire is for you, but you must master it."
> —Genesis 4:5-7 (RSV)

What we do with this manner of upset is what the story revolves around. Notice it is a perceived problem that exists only in Cain's head. He makes up a story about the god's rejection and calls it reality—just as we do daily with the happenings in our lives. Stuff happens, we create a story about it, and then we call that story the truth.

Envy can cause a positive or negative outcome. Positive reactions drive humans to strive for a better outcome. If one takes their upset and creates positively, that person (and society) gains from that upset. We call that being successful, and that is a fine quality to have in daily life. Look around at successful people today. That drive to be the best is founded on envying others' success—wishing for their success—and more. Envy, when internalized and focused on retribution, will cause destruction. Envy turns into hate and jealousy. If our upset is pointed toward the person we are angry with, envy causes destruction of the person being envied. Actions are taken to reduce that person to a level below your abilities. Today, that is called "finding the common denominator," or worse yet, "equity."

> Then the LORD said to Cain, "Why are you angry, and why is your expression downcast? Is it not true that if you do what is right, you will be fine? But if you do not do what is right, sin is crouching at the door. It desires to dominate you, but you must subdue it." —Genesis 4:6-7 (NET)

Here we see Cain's god offering advice about how to deal with envy. First off, we must notice *the god is not angry with Cain for his upset about the rejection.* Yahweh Elohim says it is up to him (Cain) to determine what to do about the upset, and how that choice will affect him (Cain) and the party he

---

2   Traditional reading likens this to something ready to pounce or invade. The Hebrew text, however, denotes this as being more of a family dog who waits patiently at the outside door to enter at his master's wish.

is upset with (Abel), who had nothing to do with Cain's upset. It is our choice only how we respond to upset, in this case, envy. If in a positive manner, we have a better life. If negatively, our lives are diminished, and we bring harm to others. Cain was upset because he made up a story. Abel won the game of offerings to the Creator God. Instead of heeding the advice given by his god, he let envy fester into anger.

Cain Chose Poorly

How could a human who did his work responsibly and cared enough to provide an offering suddenly become so base as to deprive another human of opportunity? It's a harsh question and one that has no answer. We see this occurring even to this day in the world around us.

> And the LORD said, "What have you done? The voice of your brother's blood is crying to me from the ground. And now you are cursed from the ground, which has opened its mouth to receive your brother's blood from your hand. When you till the ground, it shall no longer yield to you its strength; you shall be a fugitive and a wanderer on the earth." —Genesis 4:10–12 (RSV)

Cain, because of his actions, lost his livelihood: farming in the Garden of Eden. He was kicked out. Wait, what? How can this be reconciled with what tradition has said for eons, that this occurred outside the garden? Time is not linear for the first eleven chapters of Genesis, nor for the rest of Genesis, although in a broader sense. Just because this story followed Adam and Eve's removal does not mean it requires Cain's actions to be enacted outside of the garden. We know from the garden story that Adam was to tend the garden and that the garden had cattle inside. Cain tended the garden and Abel watched over the cattle. Cain was cursed, and his job in the garden was forbidden to him. He was told to leave, and it broke him.

> Then Cain said to YHWH, "My punishment is too great to endure! Look, you are driving me off the land today, and I must hide from your presence. I will be a homeless wanderer on the earth; whoever finds me will kill me!" But YHWH said to him, "All right then, if anyone kills Cain, Cain will be avenged seven times as much." Then YHWH put a special mark on Cain so that no one who found him would strike him down. So Cain went out from the presence of YHWH and lived in the land of Nod, east of Eden. —Genesis 4:13–16 (NET)

Cain was to leave the presence of his god, which, at that time, was in the garden. He was evicted.

After Eden

We are told Cain wandered to the east, which, in those times, meant he was headed toward a brighter future. Here we see the god offering Cain a possibility for survival. God offers to protect him after his cry of guilt. He places a mark on him to dissuade others from harming Cain, even saying it will be seven times worse for them! Seven is a potent number in this case. The number seven tells us that the life or death of Cain is up to the god. No one else gets that choice. If one ponders that for a moment, shedding someone's blood is reserved for the god's purposes, not man.[3]

Much has been pondered about what Cain's mark was. We shall never know, and that is okay, for it does not matter. Was it a tattoo or something else? Personally, I say it is a large, bright neon sign of some sort saying *do not touch*, hanging over his head. What is driving Cain's fear of death at the hands of others? If he was the firstborn child of the first humans, who is he referring to? The only possibility is of people outside the garden. We know that outside the garden there were plants and animals, birds, and fishes. What is to stop humans from being outside the garden as well? The answer is simple, for the whole of the second creation story is for the god's chosen, those who are in the garden, not those who are outside.

Cain's words are about humans, other nongarden people harming him because he is "other." Remember, this is a primordial story that creates a foundation for the Hebrews. The very next verse says that Cain and his wife fadoodled, and she bore Enoch. An oft-asked question is *where did Cain get his wife?* The most common theological answer is that it must have been Cain's sister. This makes little sense. For not too long after this we see Seth, Eve's third child, produce children. Where did *his* wife come from? And all the other wives of the descendants? We know without a doubt the god had a problem with incest, as found in the after-action account of the flood, among other stories.[4]

---

3   This does cause conflict with what the legal system in Deuteronomy states. Remember, though, it is Yahweh's ordinances, not humanity's, that give the okay to shed the blood of another.

4   Ham's incest with his mother; Lot being raped by his daughters; King David's son Amnon, who raped his sister Tamar; Reuben's incest with his father's concubine, Bilhah.

Another question, although as silly as the wife questions above, is this: Who were their parents? The answer to that question will settle many theological issues in one fell swoop. Either the parents of the wives of Seth and Cain were co-created with Adam, or they came from outside the garden. The wives of the two brothers must have been outsiders. Cain's wife was from the land of Nod, which is nowhere near what was left of the garden. Cain, once he was apart from the garden, kept farming. His first son built a city for those outside-the-garden people. Who were the inhabitants of that early metropolitan hub? Our author does not leave his audience hanging. We have to look at what is written, and we will get what he intended.

A wrap on the Abel part of the story is necessary. Abel's name in Hebrew is *Hevel*, which means "breath"—a short breath. This is our first clue about Hevel and the most telling clue because Hevel is a cipher, a necessary other, for Cain to do what he does. This story has nothing to do with Abel. We need him to make the story work. First, if there was no Abel, there would be no comparison event for Cain to be upset about. His god was the one who declined Cain's sacrifice, but Cain envied and blamed Abel. The part about the murder is an extreme example of how destructive envy can be—destructive to the person dealing with the envy and to others. That is what the author wanted his readers to know. Boy, these ancient unnamed (Baruch ben Neriah) authors were good! No, there are too many questions that arise if Cain is already outside the garden when this story happens.

Making a List—Breaking Down the Order of Events (RSV)

1. Disobedience—"Cain said to Abel his brother, 'Let us go out to the field.' And when they were in the field, Cain rose up against his brother Abel and killed him (v. 8).

2. Discovery—"Then the LORD said to Cain, 'Where is Abel your brother?' He said, 'I do not know; am I my brother's keeper?'" (v. 9).

3. Accusation—"And the LORD said, 'What have you done? The voice of your brother's blood is crying to me from the ground'" (v. 10).

4. Judgment—"And now you are cursed from the ground, which has opened its mouth to receive your brother's blood from your hand" (v. 11).

5. Punishment—"When you till the ground, it shall no longer yield to you its strength; you shall be a fugitive and a wanderer on the earth" (v. 12).

6. Leniency (mercy)—"Then the LORD said to him, 'Not so! If anyone slays Cain, vengeance shall be taken on him sevenfold.' And the LORD put a mark on Cain, lest any who came upon him should kill him" (v. 15)

This is the same thing that happened to his parents, in the same order. Eve and Adam ate from the tree, hid when their god came for coffee, and were discovered by their god, who guessed why they hid. They were told how awful it is outside the garden and then thrown out. Their god clothed them better, then sent Adam and Eve off with the original blessing intact. Time being irrelevant to this story allows for all that happened in both the second creation and Cain's debacle to occur in any order the author wanted. Cain's actions tell us of interactions of community, which, at its worst, deprive humanity of being human. This is an ultimate crime against the god, for it is his domain only. Breath is a special gift to humanity; blood keeps breath working for humanity to live. Depriving either of another human is a crime against Yahweh Elohim. For humans, taking a brother's (or sister's) life is destroying community. And yes, I mean destruction.

A Traditional View

Cain is a bad man, verboten and yucky. He killed his brother, so anything he or his progeny did was bad by default. Even though the technology introduced by Cain's outcome is fantastic and in use today, we discard it with a sniff and snort. This concept must be true, for I have heard it from the pulpit. Despite what we are led to believe, consider what technology is presented in the Cainite lineage. Cain killed his brother and was forbidden from tilling the ground (in the garden). Here we find the first technology, however crude it was. Tilling the ground (farming) requires understanding how seeds work in the ground and the creating of tools to do what that work required.

After being kicked out of the Garden of Eden, he traveled and got married and had kids. Cain's first named child (Enoch) then built the first city and named it after himself.[5] Here we find an origin; communal living equals civilization. Later kin became traveling traders. Time passed, and the making of musical instruments was added to the technological advancements. Not to be outdone, we also eventually find metalworking in brass and iron.[6] What is listed here: farming, city-dwelling, trade, music, and metalwork somehow survived through the flood. We see more aspects of subduing the earth! Yay, humans!

There is another aspect to the directive of subduing the earth to consider. We find in the Cain genealogy aspects of increasing humankind's potential, as seen above. Another reference back to the Cosmic Creator God's something special for humankind.

> Then God said, "*Let us make man in our image, after our likeness;* and let them have dominion over the fish of the sea, and over the birds of the air, and over the cattle, and over all the earth, and over every creeping thing that creeps upon the earth." So *God created man in his own image, in the image of God he created him; male and female he created them.*
> —Genesis 1:26–27 (RSV)

We are different from the beasts of the field because we can think, and, yes, like Cain, make up stories about stuff. Animals and plants cannot do this; they were not offered that promise. Dogs do what they do because they are dogs. Snakes are the way they are because that is the way snakes are. Humans are unique. They do as they choose, stupid as their choices may far too often be. Humans, made in the image of the Cosmic Creator God, can use that extra gift and create. Cain chose poorly, yet with the leniency offered by his god, he and his progeny were foundational to the future promise of his god.

As I sit here at my keyboard, I get to consider what had to be created for

---

5   Confusion abounds in the English translation, which seems to say that Cain built the first city. The Hebrew writings are not confused. Enoch is the builder of cities.

6   I find this interesting since iron-working was discovered far, far after the flood saga. Even Moses predates the discovery and use of iron!

me to write this book. What is electricity, and how did we harness that power? Or how to create plastic from sludge pulled from the earth? I write on a computer instead of a chisel and stone. I am sitting inside, comfortable while the winter storm outside slashes rain and winds against my abode, writing in a language that will spread my ideas to others, both now and in the future. I'm drinking hot coffee, whose beans were transported halfway across the world in a way that would have boggled the minds of the ancients. Yes, this is but a short list, but you are smart and get my point. Humans create stuff all the time, and it is good. Cain's lineage denotes the beginning of that wonderful process we call progress. Yet we consider the offspring of Cain beneath us. We are remiss in our assumptions; if we only look at who is in the cast of characters, we find a disturbing similarity to Adam's lineage. In Cain's lineup, there are seven people listed—nine, if Lamech's sons are included. Adam gets ten, the last being Noah. Consider the two lineages below. See the similarity?

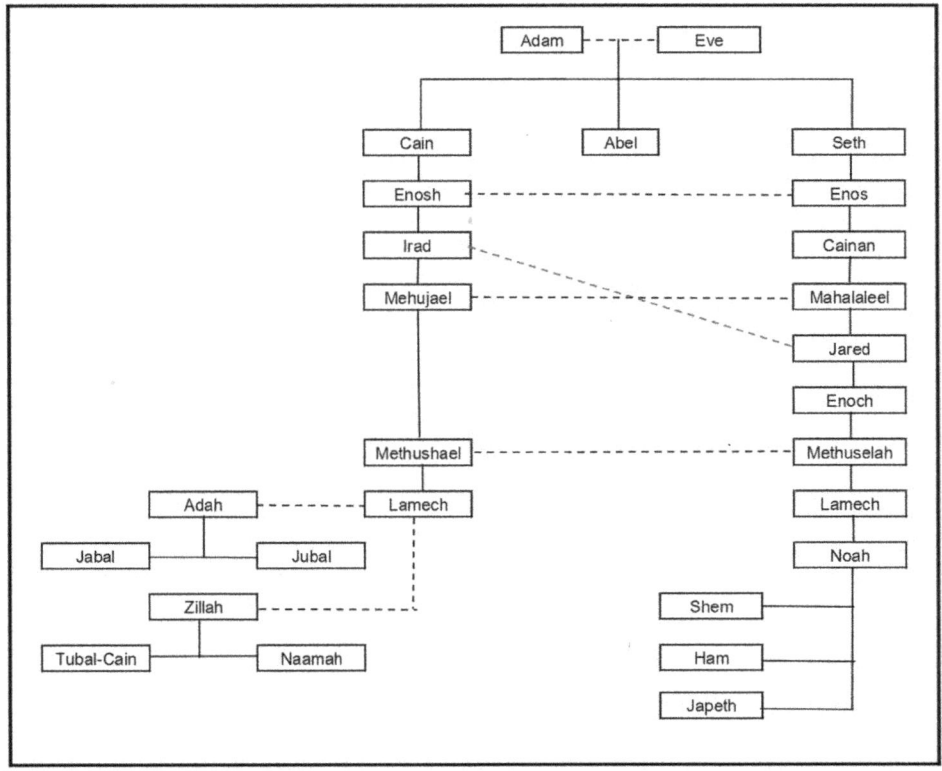

Not one scholar has spent any time considering Cain and his descendants. Cain's line is short compared to Seth's. We have no ages, for the writer cares not about this. Looking at the list above, there are possible comparisons of the lineages that correspond with each other. Name spellings were fluid, so the dotted lines likely represent the same person (or an important somebody or tribe at the time of origin). There are two people who are missing from Cain's list: Cainan and Enoch. We know nothing about Cainan, other than that he is known for his other name, Kenan. Enoch is the only one in Seth's line who has a story attached. "And Enoch walked with the god (the Elohim); and he was not; for Elohim took him."[7] It is not until we come to Cain's Lamech where we find more information about the people. Lamech marries two women, Adah and Zillah. Adah's son Jabal was the first nomad, wandering and tending to his herd. Jubal created the first harp and flute. Zillah, Lamech's other wife, had a daughter who was named Naamah, whose birth we are for some reason informed about.[8] Zillah's son, Tubal-Cain, is the first metal worker.

> Lamech took two wives for himself; the name of the first was Adah, and the name of the second was Zillah. Adah gave birth to Jabal; he was the first of those who live in tents and keep livestock. The name of his brother was Jubal; he was the first of all who play the harp and the flute. Now Zillah also gave birth to Tubal-Cain, who heated metal and shaped all kinds of tools made of bronze and iron. The sister of Tubal-Cain was Naamah. —Genesis 4:19–22 (NET)

Much scholarly time has been spent regarding the Adamic genealogy, although it is Seth's lineage that is discussed. The Cainite genealogy is as much Adamic as Seth's, but—well. Ick! Research into both lineages finds a bias. Seth's people get the nice treatment not only in Sunday school but in the actual passages. Here we find the age when the son was born and how long they lived afterward. This whole discussion is rife with supposition and scholarly conflict. The largest issue is why these ages are given. There is an answer, but no one today understands what it means. A meaning of what is the fun part, but until archaeology makes a real find, we shall never know.

---

7   Genesis 5:24 (OJB).
8   Perhaps this was Noah's wife? It would make sense, but this is only conjecture.

A Final Thought

Opposed to the traditional view, we see the author telling us of how our upsets can create a positive outcome or not. Looking past the story, we see in Cain's lineage how important this idea is, for his son Enoch created a community, a larger aspect of intimate working and living with others. How we respond to those upsets will affect not only ourselves but the entirety of those around us. Our author brilliantly offers the perspective that persons who are not of our kin are still our brothers. Also, if we take that thinking and apply it to others outside our comfort zone, the delights of community are there for all to benefit from.

A last thought for this essay: keep the story of what happened to a minimum. The god never said why Cain's offering was rejected, for it was not Cain's place to question. Intimate relations require communication. Cain's god did just that by having a conversation about Cain's story and what it could (and did) lead to.

CHAPTER 9

Kerfuffle at the River Jabbok

Brothers in Genesis are, to say the least, a handful. If they are not telling on one another to their parents, they are killing one another or selling each other into slavery. Lying and cheating are not uncommon. One must admit, however, this makes for enjoyable reading! Sadly, the literary brilliance of the actual story gets subsumed when layer and layer of meaning and theology are laid on top. When these layers are set aside, we see how such stories hold insights and features that are, frankly, so much more exciting and relevant to our lives than what is preached.

Let us make up a story about brothers. Let us make them twins. As we know, twins cannot be born together at the same time, so there will be a firstborn and the second child. Okay, no problem so far. We want a description of the two to outline our story, so let us start with the eldest twin. He will be a manly sort, outdoorsy, with red hair. He will be the one who is an all-star athlete with a positive attitude. A straightforward person who says what is on his mind, however silly it will be. We will make him rather naive and easily fooled. He will be the kid who wants to go hunting and fishing with his dad. He knows also that he will get the vast majority of his father's estate when the time comes. The second child will be a mama's boy. He needs to be sneaky and know how to make his brother look foolish. This second child also needs to be a cheat and an accomplished liar. He and his mother concoct schemes to embarrass the father and firstborn. He prefers the indoors, which distances himself from his father's love and affection. One last item: without changing who they are throughout the story, the first child will be the bad guy. His lying, cheating, thieving, and conniving brother will be the hero.

We have produced the outline of the story about Jacob and Esau. They are the sons of Isaac, whose own story will be recounted in another chapter. We will not look at the whole of their lives and the problems they had with each other, but we will focus on one aspect of their lives—an important one, the most theologically confusing one. (Uh oh, another origin story!) We see a bias regarding the two children in the story. Jacob, the younger, will become the founder of the nation of Israel, while Esau will become the founder of the nation of the Edom. There has been an enmity between the two clans throughout history. Genesis 32 provides the landscape for our Jacob and Esau periscope. We will focus on the eventful evening before their reunion after decades apart. Also, did what happened that night impact the following morning's actions? I have struggled with this episode about that night at the river Jabbok and have been eager to see if there was something missing that is in plain sight. Upon reading the story, why, yes. Yes, there is. Upon reflection and careful personality study of those two, I am confident we will see much more clearly the truth of what happened that night that will explain the next day—and how that reunion works much better in the story as well as for the future. We owe it to the writer, for he has done such masterful work to this point, keeping a tight rein on the story at this critical juncture. He certainly did, and we will honor his wishes.

Jacob and Esau

Having been estranged for over two decades, we find the two brothers about to meet in Genesis 32. At this juncture, the fate of the Abrahamic tradition will be decided, either in bloodshed or peace. Jacob is worried. He knows his brother is coming to meet him with an army. Jacob knows that neither he nor his family might be alive to see the sunset. He sends his family away and stays by the brook of Jabbok, the border of the land of his brother and freedom. We enter the story here, for here is the climax, the culmination of his sneaky, slimy, miserable, lying, wealth-accumulating life.

(Cue the flashback montage with music and funky lights.)

After fleeing Esau's wrath, Jacob worked for his uncle Laban, who, like Jacob, is full of mischief. He treats his nephew poorly. But Jacob gets two wives, two concubines, twelve sons, and assorted daughters from the arrangement. He also lies, cheats, and steals from his uncle and gains wealth. Under cover of darkness (because that is Jacob's M.O.), Jacob flees from Laban with his whole caboodle. He and his entourage are caught mid-flight by his uncle/father-in-law. They have lunch together and hug. Laban quietly tells Jacob never, ever to return.

(End of montage.)

Now we get to the good stuff. While fleeing Laban, Jacob sends messengers to Esau, telling him he is returning. Esau, by this time, had become a powerful person in his own right in the land of his father, Isaac, and Grandpa Abraham. When Esau hears of Jacob's return, he gets four hundred men (fighting men) and heads out at a gallop to meet Jacob. This size force is the standard regiment size of a raiding party, and they are headed right for Jacob and his family. Jacob, being the straightforward and honest person he is (yeah, right), divides his camp into three groups. The first group is a peace offering to Esau, full of animals and tribute, to soften his brother up. Then he divides his family and remaining assets into two other groups. The middle group contains his first wife (Leah, whom Laban tricked Jacob into marrying), his concubines, and their combined progeny. The last group has his favorite wife (Rachel), her child (Joseph), and his best possessions. Finally, being the great guy he is, he remains behind them at the ford where they crossed.

> So, Jacob was left alone. Then a man wrestled with him until daybreak. When the man saw that he could not defeat Jacob, he struck the socket of his hip, so the socket of Jacob's hip was dislocated while he wrestled with him. Then the man said, "Let me go, for the dawn is breaking." "I will not let you go," Jacob replied, "unless you bless me." The man asked him, "What is your name?" He answered, "Jacob." "No longer will your name be Jacob," the man told him, "but Israel, because you have fought with God and with men and have prevailed." Then Jacob asked, "Please tell me your name."

"Why do you ask my name?" the man replied. Then he blessed Jacob there.
—Genesis 32:24–29 (NET)

Since we are interested in what happened that night, we will consider a few translations featuring the wrestling match:

1. "*A man wrastlide with him* til to the morwetid" (Wycliffe Bible, 1382).

2. "And tarried behind hym selfe alone. And *there wrestled a man with hum* unto the breakynge of the daye" (The Great Bible, 1539).

3. "Now when Iaakob was left him selfe alone, *there wrestled a man with him* vnto the breaking of the day" (Geneva Bible, 1560).

4. "And Iacob was left alone: and there *wrestled a man with him*, vntill the breaking of the day" (King James Bible, 1611).

5. "And Jacob was left alone; and *a man wrestled with him* until the breaking of the day" (RSV).

6. "And Ya'akov was left by himself; *and there wrestled an ish* (man) with him until the shachar (dawn)" (JOV).

7. "And Jacob is left alone. Then *a man wrestled with him* until daybreak" (NET).

Here we see that Jacob wrestled with a man. Verses that go back through the history of English translations say "man." The Hebrew translation defines it using the word *ish*, which we have seen before and know it means someone who is of human persuasion. That word is what Adam was called in both creation stories. No elaboration is allowed here. A man is who Jacob wrestled with. Get this fixed in your head. But theologians, scholars, and preachers ignore the straight truth and make stuff up. I have seen this entity described as the river's daemon. Others describe it as Jacob's god. I have heard from the pulpit that it was Jesus himself! No, it was *a man, a human*. We will see why this is important later on. Any person who has heard or read the story of Jacob knows about the enmity between the two brothers that started even before their birth. Their mother, Rebekah, stated that the kids even fought while inside her during pregnancy.[1] This struggle for dominance continued

---

1   Genesis 25:22: "But the children struggled inside her, and she said, 'Why is this happening to me?'" (NET). The Hebrew word for *struggle* indicates a violent struggle, which was out of the ordinary.

(and even increased) as the story progressed. We are told the god said the younger will rule the older child, which never helps. This theme runs through the whole story.

Remember, Esau is a ruddy, hairy hunter who is, shall we say, depicted as not the brightest candle in the menorah, which fits the history of the Edomites. Jacob, his nemesis, is a smart mama's boy who lies, cheats, and steals to get what is due to Esau: his birthright and his father's blessing. Jacob's chicanery is evident in his actions throughout his part in the story. The ramifications of these issues are felt throughout the rest of the Hebrew Bible. When Jacob's crookedness toward his brother and father comes to light, he flees to his mother's homeland in the north. The north is where Laban and Rachel, his one true love, are.

WWE in Genesis!

These two (Jacob and the unidentified man) wrestled all night, until just before dawn. At this point, the "man" tried to escape, but Jacob did not let go until he knew the man's name and was blessed by the man. He got a name, but not in the way he was expecting. He was blessed by receiving a new name for himself, *Israel*, which means "always striving," always winning out against the odds. After blessing Isaac, the stranger (in a move that WWE superstar Goldberg would be proud of) jackhammers Jacob into the ground and escapes. Jacob, injured and limping, returns to his rear camp and proclaims he wrestled with God and won, which is not what happened.[2] Jacob, as we know from his back story, is a known liar. His statement is not surprising, considering. However, this little lie has big consequences, as we shall see.

The story says that immediately after Jacob rejoins his people, Esau and his warband show up. The two brothers face each other, embrace, and everything is hunky-dory. They have a picnic, and Esau offers Jacob prime real estate close to his home, which Jacob declines. Jacob and his crew move farther south, for we know that good fences make good neighbors. What is the issue here, you are wondering? Sounds like a straightforward story, right? Not so

---

2   We know this is a falsehood. Three chapters later, Yahweh informs Jacob of his name change (see Genesis 35:9–11). It is here at Bethel where Jacob commemorates this epiphany.

fast. Theologically, the whole wrestling match makes no sense. Jacob's god told him to return to his homeland, which he did. For what purpose did that god choose that night, of all nights, to beat his chosen hero to a pulp? A beating that left Jacob bloody, disheveled, and with a permanent limp? As Robbie the Robot likes to say, "This does not compute." This requires us to consider another plausible scenario, something that I think will give a pass to Jacob for that night's antics.

How many of us, on the eve of a day we know we are about to get called on the carpet, spend the night before in a deep, untroubled sleep? If the sword of Damocles is hanging over your head, do you snore away peacefully? No. We agonize over things that happened. What if we had done them differently, or perhaps not done them at all? We relate to those *in the dark hours of the night*, wrestling with "what-if"s and "why-did-I-do-that"s. With that in mind, perhaps Jacob wrestled with himself. I see his angst flooding through him as he reflects on his past. In the story, we get nothing of that. Plainly, there is a physical confrontation between Jacob and *a man*. It makes no sense in the scheme of things. Sure, he supposedly received a new name, which did not impact *his* life at that time. It became the tribe's name after Jacob died, but that is another story. A god who brutalized his hero yet praises him with a new moniker makes no sense. Jacob has more story left in him. Why harm him like that? There must be a more logical reason for the night before the meeting.

Let us consider the alien on our face that keeps us from seeing what is right in front of us. Esau had lived with a well-founded hate toward his twin his whole life, and rightfully so. Fighting in his mother's womb with his twin started the trajectory of his life. His brother stole his birthright and even tricked his father into giving Jacob Esau's blessing. We are told of his (Esau's) as well as his father's shock when they realized what had happened after Jacob's deceit. This caused Esau to plan on murdering his brother after his father died.

We know this, for it is mentioned in the story. And now we understand why Rebekah told Jacob to flee to her homeland. Esau knew where Jacob went and how his life was progressing during his time away. Esau planned revenge at the earliest available moment. Over two decades later, when Esau discovered Jacob was returning, the first thing he did was plan a war party to end the embarrassment. Removing Jacob and his tribe would ease the pain and return his firstborn birthright back to Esau, the rightful owner. The blessing his father, Isaac, was supposed to give him would then revert back to Esau. Esau also, by killing Jacob and his tribe, would stop the jokes about him being the fall guy. Plus Esau, by right, would gain all of Jacob's possessions. A total win for Esau—sucks to be you, Jacob.

A Question Answered

We must therefore ask the obvious question that is never opined about from the pulpit. Why, then, would it *not* be Esau that wrestled with his brother that night? It is obvious to whoever reads the story that Jacob was hiding behind his precious possessions to save his lying, cheating, conniving skin. Esau thought, *What better way to finish the issue than with no one knowing?* Kill that rascal Jacob in the dark of the night while he is alone, with no one to see or hear. It is right there in the words. The story, in a sneaky way, is telling us whodunnit. Another angle to consider—why did the attacker want to flee before the sun rose? Could it be so Jacob did not see it was his brother attempting to kill him? We never learn who Jacob's assailant was according to the story. Or do we? It is in the blessing that gave Jacob a new name. Esau was saying, "You fought well enough to force me to cheat, and our god will have to manage the result." Don't believe me?

> "No longer will your name be Jacob," the man told him, "but Israel,[3] because you have fought with God and with men and have prevailed." —v. 28 (NET)

Think about this series of events. The best scripts are those that tell you in obvious words but lead you to think differently. Such writing is the mark of an expert storyteller, and we have one here putting ink to paper, folks! The writer goes even further when he writes what Jacob said when he got back to his camp. Remember, Jacob is a sneaky, conniving liar. He is also a pragmatist. He knows who he fought that night and why. If, upon returning to camp, he said, "My brother attempted to kill me last night!" there would be bloodshed that day when the two brothers met. Being ever resourceful,

---

3   Hebrew: Yahweh fights.

Jacob kept his mouth shut and spouted a nonsensical reason he was lamed. Sure, make his god the reason, no one then asked the obvious question of "Wut?" It saves his ego, too, because being bested is embarrassing.

Back-to-Back, They Faced Each Other

When Esau rode up with his war party, four hundred strong, Jacob was ready to see the death and destruction of all he had labored to gain. To the surprise of everyone in the story, as well as we the readers, Esau did the honorable thing. He pretended to let bygones be bygones. Esau also knew Jacob knew who was fighting him that night. If each brother did not play the game right, bloodshed would happen. Mutually assured destruction was right there, awaiting the wrong move. Instead, we see hugging and crying and men of that age being men of that age. Jacob was able to live, and Esau was able to keep his own dynasty alive. Esau tried one last move to lure his brother into a false sense of ease by offering him land nearby, but Jacob countered gracefully by saying he wished for more free space. He did not travel with his brother south; rather, he went west. Peace was maintained—for now. However, the enmity between the two tribes would grow more and more across the ages. Read the book of Obadiah, and you will see the prophecy about their downfall because the Edomites helped the Babylonians destroy Jerusalem and the first temple.

A Satisfactory Resolution

This story, as amended, now works. The pieces fit together where they did not before—we have an origin story for the Edomites, and the mutual distrust between them and Israel is created. Read as a novel, there is intrigue and beautifully written misdirection. Jacob's lies offer a place for the writer to have fun pointing readers down the wrong path. Esau is not the naive person we are led to believe in the early part of the story; he's the actual good guy in the story who gets the raw end of the deal while Jacob gets to be the hero, despite being a lying, conniving, backstabbing trickster.[4]

Unfortunately, we see this new discovery puts the theological idea to rest.

---

4   As stated above, in chapter 35, when Yahweh changes his name to Israel, Jacob's entire demeanor transforms.

There was no god involved, just a convincing lie. This lie allowed lives to be saved and history to flow unimpeded. We can follow the story arc as written, but without considering the facts, theologians have been led astray. Accepted at face value, the falsehood by Jacob having wrestled with his god was too good for them to pass up. Trusting the word of a known liar is silly, yet they did just that. It allowed much pondering and wonderment. Here, again, I believe our late-day, tradition-bound thinking has led us down an incorrect path—one that dilutes the brilliance of the author and his end goal.

If you are not convinced yet, look at what Jacob says to his brother. Jacob is telling Esau he knows exactly who he fought that night. He spoke with words that only Esau understood. And Esau got the message. It is right there in plain sight, yet we overlook the import so quickly.

Jacob said, "No, I pray you, if I have found favor in your sight, then accept my present from my hand; *for truly to see your face is like seeing the face of God*, with such favor have you received me. Accept, I pray you, my gift that is brought to you, because God has dealt graciously with me, and because I have enough." Thus he urged him, and he took it.—v. 10-11 (RSV) We will never know who this nameless (Baruch ben Neriah) writer was. A master storyteller who knew how to tell us what we need to know yet plays with the story to deliver a successful ending. The ending is an origin story, one that explains the enmity between the Israel and Edom. The author makes the lying weasel of a guy (Jacob) into the hero. Simultaneously, he sets the stage for the actual beginning of the "rest of the story," the advent of the children of Israel from Jacob's twelve sons, the Jewish nation. What a sweet turn of events—thanks, nameless author!

Conclusion

Most telling is the old saying that goes, "Nice guys finish last." This meme permeates throughout the Tanakh. Hosea, Uriah, Ishmael, Jonathan, and so many more fall victim to bad guys winning. Another sad but true story of life. We see a continuation of the brother/brother issue, which started with Cain. The dynamic of sibling struggles inside of these stories shows how it's not just family that is involved but how the community gets sundered. It happens today. Communities, nations, regions, and, yes, families are affected in ways that are so very often started between two family rivals. World peace? Perhaps starting with our brothers will yield more in the long run.

CHAPTER 10

A Case of Mistaken Identity

We learned about Isaac's children, Jacob and Esau, in the previous chapter. In this chapter, we will consider Isaac and his brother, Ishmael. We will not be considering any antics or tomfoolery that happened between these brothers, of which there are none recorded except for one instance, and that was of an older brother being mean to a much younger one, as brothers are wont to do. (Considering the enmity between their mothers, it was a very small tiff). To take the story up a notch, these two boys are both the firstborn of the patriarch Abraham. And by both being the first child born; they will receive the blessing due to someone with that claim. No, instead, we will consider what happens to children who are brothers by another mother. These two brothers are ciphers in the entire scheme in the anthology of the patriarchs. They both have walk-on parts in this drama; their characters are not filled out with any meaningful detail.

We will focus on Genesis 22. Our periscope here will look at the *Akedah*. This is the Hebrew word for the binding of Isaac. Christian circles know it better as the time Abraham was instructed to sacrifice his firstborn son. The question is, were the players of the Akedah only Abraham, Isaac, and an angel of Yahweh? Or did the story become garbled, and the truth waylaid? We will consider why the author inserted this event where it is in the timeline. In our day and age, we view life in chronological order. Outside sources of that time reveal that chronological order is neither important nor expected. If we put chronology aside and think like the ancients, what problems that arise in the Akedah can be solved?

The Akedah

Tradition holds that thirteen years after Abraham's second firstborn son, Isaac, is born of Sarah, his first firstborn son, Ishmael, is cast out into the wilderness with his mother, Hagar. This was demanded by Sarah, Abraham's wife. Some indeterminant time after that episode, Abraham's god has a chat with Abraham and tells him to sacrifice Isaac. Abraham gets the sacrifice stuff together. With his son, they then travel for three days to where Isaac's life will end. Only here, on this part of the journey, do we hear young Isaac ask a question: "Um, Pa, we have firewood, rope, and a knife. Are we not missing something, like the animal to be killed?"

To which his father, Abraham, replied, "Our god will sort it out, I expect."[1] Which is what happened. Abraham's god got it all sorted and saved Isaac. Thank goodness for angels and a proper animal for sacrifice standing by in the wings.

Theologians have had a field day expounding on what this story is about. However, its placement in the storyline makes no logical sense, much like the kerfuffle at Jabbok. I have heard hours of sermons and read countless religious and critical books surrounding this event, and none of them have passed the sniff test. Perhaps it is good that I am not a theologian, for this story does not fit the theology. For me, the writer had this story on hand and did not know where to put it, so he plopped it down at the end because, well, it had to go somewhere.

The ancient writers threw nothing away. There had to be something fishy about the original story to begin with. Logic wrinkles its nose; the puzzle pieces do not match up. Abraham has two firstborn children. Each child received the same promise of a nation from their loins. Now Abraham's god is telling him to kill one of the kids? Placement of this story does not line up.

---

1   Every time I read this, I hear Andy and Opie's voices from *Mayberry R.F.D.*

It is misaligned to anything the author has produced so far. We hear nothing from Sarah in this section, which is unusual. She is the lead in this drama. For her to be ignored does not work. Is there a solution to these problems? Yes, of course! Here is what I have found via a close reading of the texts and also by recognizing human nature, which has not changed since the dawn of time.

Ishmael and Isaac

I realize that since the story of Ishmael and Isaac is before the Jacob and Esau story, this should have been touched on first. However, as we will see, putting things in order was not a priority in the days of Abraham and his press agent. Do not be surprised by this, for as we will discover, the order of events is crucial to our discovery! The actors in this drama are Abraham, his wife, Sarah, and Sarah's slave, Hagar. They are the people who will be up for the Academy Awards. Of the two kids, Ishmael and Isaac, only one has a spoken line. A single spoken line. Ishmael and Isaac will get their own more active roles later, after the Akedah—we have that to look forward to. People will be surprised to find Abraham is the foil of this multi-act drama. Sarah, his wife, has the lead role. The supporting cast is Sarah's slave, Hagar.

Making Babies

As is typical of Hebrew females, a patriarch's wife who is unable to bear a child would beseech Yahweh Elohim and promise something to the god. Sarah, the lead character in our story, starts us off in this lineup. Rebekah, Isaac's wife, has twins, one of whom is our loveable rascal, Jacob. Jacob's favorite wife, Rachel, eventually has two, one of which will become second only to the pharaoh of Egypt. Samson's mother is on the list, as is Samuel the prophet's mother.[2] We find Elizabeth, the mother of John the Baptist, barren as well. These women were unable to bear children until an intervention of their god, with wonderful outcomes to history as we know it today.

Backstory

We turn now to Sarah, ten years younger than Abraham. Throughout the story, Sarah was known as Sarai, and Abraham's moniker was Abram. (The

---

2   Samuel was instrumental in creating kingship throughout the land. He is accorded two books with his name.

name change occurs later and is important to our story.) Sarai cannot get pregnant. She will eventually tell Hagar to become Abram's concubine. Hagar, of course, gives birth to Ishmael. Eventually, Sarah will give birth to a son by Abraham. That son will be Isaac, who will be cast in a walk-on role in the Akedah. That is the shortest summation of what is transpiring to get to the climax of this consideration. We must consider the backstory as well as rather simple statements during that chronology that are overlooked (yet will tell us so much).

Both Sarai and Abram started their life together far south in the land of Mesopotamia, in the city of Ur.[3] In the story, their god told Abram to move to the complete opposite end of Mesopotamia, to the place called Haran.[4] They moved, and prospered, for Haran was a trading center at the crossroads for traffic from as far south as Egypt, as far north as Anatolia, as far west as what became India, as well as from around the Mediterranean Sea. Abram was seventy years old when they arrived in Haran.

At seventy-five, their god gave Abram a promise to build a vast nation from his seed if they moved again, but south along the eastern coast of the Mediterranean Sea. They packed up and headed south. Sarai, we are told, is a good-looking woman, especially for her age, which gets both Abram and the pharaoh of Egypt into trouble while they were wandering around Canaan and Egypt waiting for their god to say, "Stop." I find this intriguing. The couple's antics during their sojourn make for fun reading and add to Abraham's wealth and status. This was their god's way of ensuring resources for the nation-building that was to come. At age 85, Abram and Sarai (age 75) are re-promised the child that had not appeared. Sarai is tired of waiting and forms a plan to get the party started. She concocts an idea and presents it to her husband.

> Now Sarai, Abram's wife, had not given birth to any children, but she had an Egyptian servant named Hagar. So Sarai said to Abram, "Since the LORD has prevented me from having children, please sleep with my servant. Perhaps I can have a family by her." Abram did what Sarai told him . . . He slept with Hagar, and she became pregnant. —Genesis 16:1–4 (NET)

---

3 Ur is very close to where our flood story originated in Mesopotamia.
4 Haran was at a major crossroads for the trade routes.

This type of thing was not unusual during this time. Having a surrogate produce an heir, or even buying a child, was fair game. That child, if no official offspring arrived, would have the rights accorded as the firstborn. Sarai would get the credit, even though Hagar did the work. Of course, as we rightly expect in a Bible story, problems arise instantly between the two women, and Sarai takes it out on Abram as though it were his fault!

> Once Hagar realized she was pregnant, she despised Sarai. Then Sarai said to Abram, "You have brought this wrong on me! I gave my servant into your embrace,[5] but when she realized that she was pregnant, she despised me. May the LORD judge between you and me!" Abram said to Sarai, "Since your servant is under your authority, do to her whatever you think best." Then Sarai treated Hagar harshly, so she ran away from Sarai.
> —Genesis 16:4–6 (NET)

What is a guy to do? And now you see why I said Abram is the foil. Sarai is upset, and she took it out on Abram—not because he got Hagar pregnant but because of her attitude. Sarai, with her husband's approval, kicked Hagar and Abram's (first) firstborn out to the curb. The result of this upset is a wonderful story about Hagar—after a conversation with an angel of Abram's god, she returns to her mistress. But during that conversation with the angel, Hagar receives a promise that her child, Ishmael, would "multiply your descendants exceedingly, so that they shall not be counted for multitude" (NKJV). Here we have the origin story of Islam, which calls Ishmael the father of their belief. Also, this is the tie-in for how they view Islam's connection to the Abrahamic tradition. Abram was eighty-six years old when Ishmael was born and became Abram's official firstborn. This only-son thing lasted thirteen years. During this time, the enmity between Ishmael's mother and her mistress grew uglier, as expected. Luckless Ishmael grew into a rowdy young man, even though his mother had a promise from the angel. What a life sentence for the bit player in a story that has eternal ramifications. He was his father's firstborn and yet relegated to secondary status from birth.

Finally, when Abram was ninety-nine years old, His god finally got face-to-face with Abram and Sarai and sealed the covenant of creating a dynasty. Their god took the promise further this time. He gave both Abram and Sarai

---

5   Hebrew: Your lap.

updated names that were an outward expression of the covenant. What he did was add an *H* to their names. This rather simple deed had huge import in their situation in life. That letter was part of their god's name. Having such tokens was big stuff in that setting in life—big stuff. One other ritual requirement came into being: the last part of the covenant was that males of Abraham's family were to be circumcised. Yes, this is where that whole deal came from. Consider that to be as credible as Cain's mark, although in a positive manner. Do not mess with Abraham, Sarah, or their family, for they are the Cosmic Creator God's elected representatives.

With the covenant and name changes now in place, Sarah got pregnant. No, not right away, for we see side quests for Abraham and Sarah that preceded the conception. One has to do with a nephew of Abraham—Lot. Lot gets in with an unbelievably bad crowd. Despite Abraham's attempt to avert disaster, the people of Sodom and Gomorrah got burned up.[6] And then Lot's daughters did the nasty with their father,[7] but those tales are for another day. We also find Abraham and Sarah playing the pharaoh gambit again with King Abimelech, who gets caught fancying Sarah (who was still a good-looking woman, at the age of almost ninety!). This last act added much to the fortunes of Abraham and sealed a positive relationship with that powerful ruler.

Again, keeping a linear sequence is not important to ancient writers. We next see Sarah giving birth to a son, Isaac (Abraham's second firstborn). Abraham was now a centenarian, and Sarah had given him his second official firstborn. Life was good, and the stage was set for a happy ending, right?

> Sarah saw the son of Hagar the Egyptian, whom she had borne to Abraham, playing[8] with her son Isaac. So, she said to Abraham, "Cast out this slave woman with her son, for the son of this slave woman shall not inherit along with my son Isaac." The matter was very distressing to Abraham on account

6   An origin story explaining (1) the harsh environs of the Dead Sea and (2) what happens from the extreme moral depravity of not treating guests well.

7   Another origin story: the two boys that resulted from the incest are the origins of the tribes of Moab and Ammon, both wildly unpopular with Israel. This tidbit makes the story of Ruth even tastier, since she is from Moab, yet she gets to be King David's grandmother and is in Matthew's lineage of Jesus!

8   In Hebrew, this word uses the root of Isaac, which indicates whom Ishmael is focusing on. The verb is "to jest; make sport of; play with." Whatever the meaning, Sarah took offense. Also, many translations use *mock* as their descriptor.

of his son (Ishmael). But God said to Abraham, "Do not be distressed because of the boy and because of your slave woman; whatever Sarah says to you, do as she tells you, for it is through Isaac that offspring shall be named for you. As for the son of the slave woman, I will make a nation of him also, because he is your offspring." —Genesis 21:9–13 (RSV)

Let us consider this from Sarah's point of view. She has wandered a long way from her home in Ur. She has put up with Abraham for two thousand miles and traveled halfway across her known world. Sarah had been used as a pawn in several of Abraham's schemes. She has been promised a child the whole time, *especially* for the last quarter century. She rid herself of her pseudo-progeny once, and it came back to her. Now she is putting her foot down for the last time, for it is time for *her* child to shine. More to the point, it is Sarah's time for the spotlight. Her henpecked husband has been agreeable to the idea it has been his fault since we see no accounting of Abraham showing any spine. Sarah presents her ultimatum to Abraham again. He agrees to the removal of his (first) firstborn and baby mama. I do not think Sarah knows of Abraham's god promising that Ishmael and Hagar will be taken care of because Ishmael is still the firstborn. For the second time, Abraham kicks his firstborn and Hagar out. After another successful rescue story, they both live good lives.

The Real Reason

In the intervening years, from Ishmael's conception to Isaac's birth, we hear nothing about the disputes between the mothers. Strange, is it not? That such a hot internecine war is ignored? What does any of this have to do with the Akedah? Dear reader, names were changed—not to protect the innocent, as Sgt. Joe Friday used to say, but to make the story about the firstborn child that mattered in the whole history arc of the Hebrew people. The Akedah was originally placed somewhere in the sequence of events prior to Isaac being born. In its proper location, it is Ishmael to be sacrificed. Whoever the redactor was, redacted and moved this part of the play because it took the story in places he did not wish to go. We are concerned with the future of Isaac, a patriarch of the children of Israel, not Ishmael. We see our focus being shifted away from the obvious squabble. The Akedah fits best during the thirteen years between Ismael's birth and Isaac's appearance on the scene. Did Abraham have Ishmael only for progeny, to be used as a get-out-of-jail-free card? For the Akedah to fit in the storyline, it has to be set at the time that Abraham had only one child. Ishmael is a living human being destined for greatness, yet Abraham's god tells him Ishmael is to be sacrificed. Abraham was (mostly) confident his god would keep his promise to have a kid via Sarah. However, he only has one hole card. And he is asked to discard that card and hope for the luck of the draw.

> God said, "Take your son—your *only* son, whom you love, *Isaac*, and go to the land of Moriah. Offer him up there as a burnt offering on one of the mountains which I will indicate to you." —Genesis 22:2 (NET)

We see two words that show this is a gloss. You cannot have "only" preceding "*son*" in the same sentence as "Isaac." Isaac was not the only son at the time when the story was placed. We read of thirteen years when there was only one son. That son was Ishmael. The original author knew of only one son at the point where the story was written. Sorry folks, the word of the day is *one*. Abraham got tested by his god—a lot. The Akedah is one of these tests. Consider which is harder: to remove the only living, breathing son and a probable/almost-certain other child, or to remove one of a matched set who have the same promise of a future? Choose and be satisfied with your choice.

Tradition tells us Abraham loved his son Isaac. Nowhere do we find any love toward Ishmael. As to whom Abraham loved, Ishmael or Isaac, that is easy to prove. A son unloved by his father will, even in that ancient of days, will never do honor to his father or his memory. What we see, however, is upon Abraham's death, Isaac and Ishmael came together and buried their father beside Isaac's mother with full honors. Do not con me and say Abraham loved just one of his sons or did not do the best possible for either of them. The honor shown at Abraham's burial showed respect, admiration, and love both for their father and the same love and respect for each other.

Conclusion

So many origin stories presented to us! How did those ancient myths begin to insert themselves into the Hebrew psyche? Now we know! Moab and

Ammon tribal hatred? Got that in one. Is the Dead Sea a bad place to live? Yeah. Our introduction to Haran, where Jacob flees from his irate brother is here. And the Akedah is plunked down in a place that increase the tension of the story, yet fills the promise offered in a way never before appreciated.

CHAPTER 11

Joe and His Bros

The story of Joseph, which is also found in Genesis, is probably the best-written epic found in the whole of both testaments. Who wrote it (Baruch ben Neriah) is unknown, for he did not autograph the work. I blame his publisher for that. Two of the most important details for a great story are found inside this work. Writers know the main premise of a good story is that Something Goes Wrong. We find this in spades as we read about Joseph, for stuff goes wrong at almost every turn for our hero. The second aid for the writer is to be unpredictable. Again, what happens to Joseph and how he deals with all the wrongness is delightful and surprising. And this is detailed in just over 8,500 words. His story invites and pulls the reader along, teasing the mind with an ever-present *what's going to happen next?* With every word, the author ignites our imagination.

However, this chapter will focus only on one section, a part of the narrative that has ever been a thorn in my side. Our consideration will be centered upon how Joseph started his journey to Egypt. Preachers and Sunday school teachers love to preach and teach about this section in only one way, and that is how much Joseph's brothers got paid for Joseph. Never mind who took Joseph to Egypt. Or how the two brothers named are involved. We never hear the truth about why Joseph's brothers were so unhappy with him.

Also, why *are* two named brothers mentioned doing the same thing? This is an important set of questions and will be resolved.

First or Last

Our first quest is to find out why the brothers are so upset at Joseph. This is another part of the ever-present Genesis question—why are brothers so angry at each other? In this story, we learn Joseph is the firstborn of Rachel, the woman Joseph's father loved to the point of dissing his other wife, Leah: "And his love for Rachel was greater than his love for Leah."[1] This is important, for we find Rachel and Joseph are thought of much higher than any of the other wives, concubines, or sons. The first part of Genesis 37 starts our story with a basic outline of Joseph, his father, and his brothers.

With that in mind, we begin our journey. Joseph was seventeen years old at this point in the story. He was his father's favorite son. He spent his time observing his brothers and telling his father, Jacob, about their doings. In today's vernacular, the proper description is *narcing on them.* Think about this for a moment. The youngest brother tells his dad what stuff is happening, and most certainly, the rest of the brothers get into trouble. As brothers go, they are unhappy. Especially when that brat gets an article of clothing (a multicolored robe, we are told) for no good reason, proving yet again that he has his dad's ear, and his dad will believe anything Joseph says against the rest. He made up stories of his "dreams," which put the brothers on edge because the dreams were obviously about how much better Joseph was than them (the dreams relegated the brothers to submissive roles).

Let us be honest here: Joseph is a jerk to his brothers. Yet this does not give us enough information to explain why their anger burned so effervescently toward their youngest brother.[2] We must look farther into the past to get the real import of this issue. For that, we turn again to the story of when Jacob and his brother Esau were to meet after years apart. Genesis 33 tells us what is necessary. As Jacob's long-estranged brother, Esau, approached, Jacob put his concubines out front with their kids (Bilhah with Dan and

---

1   Genesis 29:30.
2   Actually, Benjamin was the youngest brother, but he does not appear in this discussion.

Naphtali, Zilpah with Gad and Asher). He positioned Leah with her kids next (Reuben, Simeon, Levi, Judah, Issachar, and Zebulun). The final group was Rachel and Joseph. Each group also had their daughters, and the slaves dedicated to the mothers. Esau would have to go through all these people before finding Jacob, who himself stayed farther back.

Imagine this scene. In one fell swoop, the mothers and sons knew exactly where they ranked in the food chain of Jacob's thinking. If Esau was bent on destruction, they would fall to the sword first. Rachel and Jacob would be the last. Perhaps Esau's bloodlust would be sated by the time those two people ended up at sword point. Joseph was about seven at the time, and Reuben, Jacob's eldest, would have been somewhere in his twenties. This means all the brothers were old enough to realize their lack of worth to their father. To say their father's actions caused mental issues is putting it mildly.

Fortunately, the whole kerfuffle at the river Jabbok ended well, and all lived.[3]

A Pit Stop

Fast-forward ten years to the time when the brothers saw Joseph coming to see them as his father had requested. Here is the kid who was apple of their dad's eye, out to spy on them—and also to tell them how much better a son he was than them. What we find next is found in the following verses of Genesis 37.

> They (Joseph's brothers) saw him from a distance, and before he came near to them they conspired to kill him. They said to one another, "Here comes this dreamer (Joseph). Come now, let us kill him and throw him into one of the pits; then we shall say that a wild animal has devoured him, and we shall see what will become of his dreams."
>
> But when Reuben heard it, he delivered him out of their hands, saying, "Let us not take his life." Reuben said to them, "Shed no blood; throw him into this pit here in the wilderness but lay no hand on him"—that he might rescue him out of their hand and restore him to his father. So when Joseph came to his brothers, they stripped him of his robe, the ornamented robe that he wore, and they took him and threw him into a pit. The pit was empty; there was no water in it. Then they sat down to eat, and looking up they saw

---

3   See the chapter "Kerfuffle at the River Jabbok."

a caravan of Ishmaelites coming from Gilead, with their camels carrying gum, balm, and resin, on their way to carry it down to Egypt.

Then Judah said to his brothers, "What profit is it if we kill our brother and conceal his blood? Come, let us sell him to the Ishmaelites and not lay our hands on him, for he is our brother, our own flesh." And his brothers agreed. When some Midianite traders passed by, they drew Joseph up, lifting him out of the pit, and sold him to the Ishmaelites for twenty pieces of silver. And they took Joseph to Egypt.

When Reuben returned to the pit and saw that Joseph was not in the pit, he tore his clothes. He returned to his brothers and said, "The boy is gone, and I, where can I turn?" Then they took Joseph's robe, slaughtered a goat, and dipped the robe in the blood. They had the ornamented robe taken to their father, and they said, "This we have found; see now whether it is your son's robe or not." He recognized it and said, "It is my son's robe! A wild animal has devoured him; Joseph has surely been torn to pieces."

Then Jacob tore his garments and put sackcloth on his loins and mourned for his son many days. All his sons and all his daughters sought to comfort him, but he refused to be comforted and said, "No, I shall go down to Sheol to my son, mourning." Thus, his father bewailed him. Meanwhile the Midianites had sold him in Egypt to Potiphar, one of Pharaoh's officials, the captain of the guard. —vv. 18–36 (RSV)

The Traditional Approach

The brothers took Joseph, tore off his fancy-schmancy robe, and dumped him in an empty pit. They sat down to eat. While eating, they saw some traders and sold Joseph into slavery for an amount of money that is not actually stated. A brother who did not seem to be present for the pit maneuver returned and expressed agony for the other brothers' deed. The brothers then took the robe back to their father with a whopper of a story. Their father Jacob promptly had a meltdown of epic proportions.

Troubling Tidbits

Read the story again, several times if you need. On its face, the traditional approach is clear, especially as preached from the pulpit (my father included). However, even as a young person, I saw problems inside the story. Somehow Judah and Reuben were the only named brothers in this story. Added to that, they appeared to be doing and saying the same thing.

Reuben: "Let us not take his life."

Judah: "And not lay our hands on him."

Whom exactly did the brothers sell Joesph to—the Ishmaelites (coming from Gilead, on their way to Egypt), or the Midianites (Midianite traders passed by)? At one point in the story, both the Midianites and the Ishmaelites are included in the same sentence (Midianites drew Joseph up and sold him to the Ishmaelites). Lest we forget to notice such little details, the Ishmaelites got paid the money, yet it was the Midianites who took him to Egypt. Or was it the other way around?

For goodness' sake, something is going on here. Why has no one noticed this? We notice a lot of pits mentioned in the story—why is this so? As I grew older, this pit story reminded me of someone else in the Bible, if I could only remember who, and what it was about.

Family Ties

In order of appearance, we find Reuben, the Ishmaelites, the Midianites, and Judah. Perhaps if we were to delve into these people, we might find something to help this conundrum. Reuben is the firstborn of Jacob by Leah. This guy has absolutely no love lost for his brother Joseph. And yet, he was able to convince his other brothers not to kill Joseph, but to put him in an available hole so he (Reuben) could save and return Joseph to his father. For some reason, Reuben left his brothers, and when he returned, Joseph was gone. Reuben's plan for Joseph was destroyed, and his life went wonky. He tore his clothes and cried, "The boy is gone, and I, where can I turn?" It is understandable, since he is the eldest. He is responsible for his siblings' well-being, and his father would hold him accountable.

We look next to the Ishmaelites, a tribe from the southern part of Canaan. If we step into the way-back machine, we see the brothers had a daddy, Jacob. Jacob had a daddy also—Isaac. Isaac was firstborn to Abraham, the guy who started this whole thing. If you remember, Abraham had another firstborn son, Ishmael. The people in our story are cousins to our brothers who are currently under the microscope. If we take the story literally, the Ishmaelites would have known the guys who had Joseph in a pit. I will put it a bit more succinctly for you Dallas Cowboys fans—they were second-cousins, and they knew it was Joseph in that hole.

Family ties are so fun to understand in the Tanakh, are they not? Our next people to look at are family also. We saw Abraham's name come up with the Ishmaelites. Guess who is responsible for the Midianites? Yes, Abraham. Abraham remarried after his wife of a million years, Sarah, passed away. He married Keturah after Sarah and fathered Zimran, Jokshan, Medan, *Midian*, Ishbak, and Shuah.[4] Here we see the origin of the clan Midian, those guys who also came along and took Joseph to Egypt. Second-cousins also, these Midianites. They are guaranteed to have known the brothers and the guy in the hole, Joseph.

Last, but certainly not least, is Judah, the fourth son of Leah, Jacob's first wife. He would have been old enough to remember the kerfuffle at the river Jabbok and understand where he stood in the line of importance to his father. Here again, there was no love lost toward Joseph, that smarmy bro of his. Yet as we see in the story, he said and did the same thing as his older brother Reuben did. (Do not kill the brat, throw him in a hole and sell Joe to slavers). Opposed to Reuben, Judah appears to have stayed for the strip show and pit maneuver.

Those silly boys, Reuben and Judah. Did their actions have any ramifications later in life? As for Reuben, his father did hold him responsible when the time came for blessings, but it was not for this issue.

> Reuben, you are my first-born, my might, and the first fruits of my strength, pre-eminent in pride and pre-eminent in power. Unstable as water, you shall not have pre-eminence because you went up to your father's bed; then you defiled it—you went up to my couch! —Genesis 49:3–4 (RSV)

This is in reference to Genesis 35.

---

4   Genesis 25:1–4.

> While Israel (Jacob) was living in that land (Migdal Eder), Reuben went to bed with Bilhah, his father's concubine, and Israel (Jacob) heard about it.
> —v. 22 (NET)

Due to his life going wonky there at the pit, Reuben lost his firstborn status, which went to another brother. Of course he would have sex with his step-mommy. *Ew!* Not to be outdone, Judah told his brother, "Hold my beer," and had sex with his daughter.[5] Surprisingly, this did not seem to affect Judah at the time of blessing.

> Judah, your brothers will praise you; your hand will be on the neck of your enemies; your father's sons will bow down to you. ... The scepter will not depart from Judah, nor the ruler's staff from between his feet, until he to whom it belongs shall come and the obedience of the nations shall be his.
> —Genesis 49:8–10 (NET)

Despite his familial dalliance, Judah got first billing in the son lottery—he ended up with firstborn status. Not to mention, the son he had with his daughter,[6] Perez, would be in the lineage of King David and Jesus of Nazareth.

No, I have not forgotten my concern regarding the pit. I have dialed it down to the Old Testament and am fairly certain the author's style is familiar to us.

A Story in a Story

What if we played the *What If* game? Suppose there were two different stories smooshed together. What if the original compiler created the original storyline, and a redactor came along—oh, say a hundred years later, and put another, similar story inside? What a surprise *that* would be, since we have only seen it a million times so far in Genesis.[7] Fortunately, baseball season is over, and I have nothing better to do. I therefore did the heavy lifting so you will not have to. I broke the story listed above into two narrations, each from the two brothers' viewpoint. What follows is the Reuben story first, since he is the firstborn. Next up will be the Judah part.

- **Reuben's Excuse:**

---

5   Genesis 38 clues us in to this sordid tale.

6   Yes, I know. Tamar was his daughter-in-law, but still.

7   I apologize. Sometimes my inside words become outside words.

They (Joseph's brothers) saw him from a distance, and before he came near to them they conspired to kill him. But when Reuben heard it, he delivered him out of their hands, saying, "Let us not take his life." Reuben said to them, "Shed no blood; throw him into this pit here in the wilderness but lay no hand on him"—that he might rescue him out of their hand and restore him to his father. and they took him and threw him into a pit. The pit was empty; there was no water in it.

Then they sat down to eat. When some Midianite traders passed by, they drew Joseph up, lifting him out of the pit. When Reuben returned to the pit and saw that Joseph was not in the pit, he tore his clothes. He returned to his brothers and said, "The boy is gone, and I, where can I turn?" Meanwhile the Midianites had sold him in Egypt to Potiphar, one of Pharaoh's officials, the captain of the guard.

- **Judah's Side:**
They said to one another, "Here comes this dreamer (Joseph). Come now, let us kill him and throw him into one of the pits; then we shall say that a wild animal has devoured him, and we shall see what will become of his dreams." So when Joseph came to his brothers, they stripped him of his robe, the ornamented robe that he wore, and looking up they saw a caravan of Ishmaelites coming from Gilead, with their camels carrying gum, balm, and resin, on their way to carry it down to Egypt.

Then Judah said to his brothers, "What profit is it if we kill our brother and conceal his blood? Come, let us sell him to the Ishmaelites and not lay our hands on him, for he is our brother, our own flesh." And his brothers agreed. and sold him to the Ishmaelites for twenty pieces of silver. And they took Joseph to Egypt.

Then they took Joseph's robe, slaughtered a goat, and dipped the robe in the blood. They had the ornamented robe taken to their father, and they said, "This we have found; see now whether it is your son's robe or not." He recognized it and said, "It is my son's robe! A wild animal has devoured him; Joseph has surely been torn to pieces." Then Jacob tore his garments and put sackcloth on his loins and mourned for his son many days. All his sons and all his daughters sought to comfort him, but he refused to be comforted and said, "No, I shall go down to Sheol to my son, mourning." Thus his father bewailed him.

What Did We Find?

Breaking the story apart gives us new insights into the story. As we can see, two distinct writers had input. Reuben's storyline reminds me again of Sgt. Joe Friday's comment, "Just the facts, ma'am." Judah's response is laden with emotion and fills our minds with color and detail. Here, again, we see our two favorite writers strutting their stuff. Ezra does the work for Reuben. Baruch ben Neriah, as always, gives a master class in writing in the Judah section.[8] Although Ezra was a century later with his redaction of Baruch, he is able to merge two stories into a whole. Yes, the redaction is rather clunky, but unless one reads very critically, a simple reading allows for a seamless tale. Now, however, we have a pleasant and uncomplicated understanding of how Joseph got to Egypt. We also get a glimpse of the great tension underlying throughout the story, and its release when Joseph and his father finally reunite in Egypt.[9]

> Then Joseph prepared his chariot and went up to meet Israel his father in Goshen. He presented himself to him and fell on his neck and wept on his neck a good while. Israel said to Joseph, "Now let me die, since I have seen your face and know that you are still alive." —Genesis 46:29–30 (ESV)

First Rule of Holes

In the case of our story, I am disregarding the first rule of holes. That rule is this: *if you find yourself in a hole, stop digging.* Yes, putting Joseph in a hole to keep him from running away is good, but what about a rope, handcuffs, or even duct tape to do the work instead? Let us apply some logic to this situation and see how far we can get for how holes work.

Put that creep Joe in a hole to die. Go back to Dad and tell him a wild animal had lunch. First problem: If the pit was deep enough to keep Joseph in,

---

8   I love how these two writers work together so well, especially living a century apart.

9   Personally, this ranks much higher than the ending of *Planes, Trains, and Automobiles*, which is the ultimate homecoming scene produced today.

the hole would, by necessity, be deep enough to keep the predator inside also. Next, for this to work in normal situations, their father would require proof. Proof in this circumstance would mean killing the lion or tiger or bear (oh, my!) and dragging its carcass along with Joseph's remains to their father. Not so in this story.

In our literature of today, we find this suspension of reason as the norm. We often read of the hero being oblivious to what is obvious to the reader. How dare we consider ancient authors unable to do great work. As it was then, so it is today. Good stuff!

What Is in a Word?

A common translation uses the word *pit or well* for the hole Joseph was put in. What confused me was this statement, hidden in plain sight: "one of the." In this part of the world, people did not go around digging holes higgledy-piggledy and leaving them open for people, animals, or Cubs fans to fall into. But the story insists there were plenty laying around. I found a few English translations that offered the word *cistern*, which is, of course, a large pot dug into the ground and used to store water. Cisterns, where found, are often in groups. Here we find the term "one of the" giving us a large clue. And that is where the lightbulb went off. I remembered a sermon my father had preached regarding not the story of a pit but of a cistern.[10]

Flipping over to Jeremiah 38, we find Jeremiah doing his thing, which is to upset and unsettle the power structure in Jerusalem by preaching destruction to everyone in the city. Let us take a step back and ponder Jeremiah. Jeremiah was special, very special. Called of Yahweh, Jeremiah's purpose in life was to be inside the city of Jerusalem and (I do not dare to use the proper words here) create havoc to the psyches of the powerful in the city. This, of course, included the king, Zedekiah. Jeremiah especially liked to find the kids of his betters and rant and rave in front of them. This scheme was quite effective, for one day Jeremiah did his thing in front of Zedekiah's son Malkijah. Malkijah of course, went running to daddy.

So these officials said to the king, "This man must be put to death. For he is

---

10   Yes, preachers' kids do occasionally listen to their father's sermons.

demoralizing the soldiers who are left in the city as well as all the other people there by these things he is saying. This man is not seeking to help these people but is trying to harm them." King Zedekiah said to them, "Very well, you can do what you want with him. For I cannot do anything to stop you."

So the officials took Jeremiah and put him in the cistern of Malkijah, one of the royal princes, that was in the courtyard of the guardhouse. There was no water in the cistern, only mud. So when they lowered Jeremiah into the cistern with ropes he sank in the mud. —Genesis 38:4–6 (NET)

Jeremiah (Joseph) was thrown into a pit (cistern) by his fellow Jerusalemites (brothers) with the intent he should die there.

To finish the story, Jeremiah was rescued by an unknown character using the alias Ebed-Melech, which means "the king's servant." Anyone who knows the story of Jeremiah will understand the double meaning of this name and who the actual person was who did the rescue. Yes, it was our unknown author, Baruch ben Neriah! Jeremiah and Baruch were the king's servants during this time. The king referenced was their god, Yahweh. Later in Jeremiah's story, he and Baruch were forced to flee to Egypt after the destruction of Jerusalem.

Tying a Pretty Bow

Richard Elliot Friedman, in his book *Who Wrote the Bible?*,[11] makes the claim that Baruch ben Neriah was the author of Deuteronomy through 2 Kings. I believe he wrote much more. We have seen Baruch's hand in the work of Genesis as well. The story of Joseph was required for the children of Israel to get to Egypt, arranging for the next epic in the cycle, Exodus. Why not use the antics of Jeremiah as a template to create the majestic Joseph epic to do that very thing? Our favorite storyteller, Baruch, is comfortable using what is at hand to create a wonderful pathway for Jacob, who lost his most beloved son, to finally reunite with Joseph in Egypt. He even promises a peaceful death with Joseph at his side.

So Israel (Jacob) began his journey, taking with him all that he had. When he came to Beer Sheba he offered sacrifices to the God of his father Isaac. God spoke to Israel in a vision during the night and said, "Jacob, Jacob!" He

---

11   See the bibliography for information on this wonderful work.

replied, "Here I am!" He said, "I am God, the God of your father. Do not be afraid to go down to Egypt, for I will make you into a great nation there. I will go down with you to Egypt and I myself will certainly bring you back from there. Joseph will close your eyes." —Genesis 46:1–4 (NET)

As Paul Harvey was known to say, "Now we know the rest of the story."

Items of Interest

To write this chapter, an understanding of who was involved required me to delineate who was a mother to Jacob's children, and in what order the children appear. What their names meant can also be important to the story, and I have listed them also. Two tidbits of interest are included at the end.

- Leah (weary/grieved), Jacob's first wife

    1—Reuben (behold, a son)

    2—Simeon (God hears)

    3—Levi (joined)

    4—Judah (let him [God] be praised)

    9—Issachar (man of hire)

    10—Zebulun (dwelling)

    ?—Dinah (judgement); daughter, birth order unspecified

- Zilpah (a drop), Rachel's slave

    5—Dan (judge)

    6—Naphtali (my wrestling)

- Rachel (ewe), Jacob's second wife, whom he loved the most

    11—Joseph (may God add)

    12—Benjamin (son of the right hand)

- Bilhah (trouble/calamity), Leah's slave

    7—Gad (good fortune)

    8—Asher (happy)

Other Notes of Interest

1. Dinah is the only sister mentioned. She gets raped, and her brothers Simeon and Levi avenge her in a most sneaky and graphic way. Genesis 34 is where that action takes place. These two brothers find their revenge antics are not well thought of when they are blessed by their father.

   > Simeon and Levi are brothers, weapons of violence are their knives! O my soul, do not come into their council, do not be united to their assembly, my heart, for in their anger they have killed men, and for pleasure they have hamstrung oxen. Cursed be their anger, for it was fierce, and their fury, for it was cruel. I will divide them in Jacob and scatter them in Israel. —Genesis 49:5–7 (NET)

   Simeon, when the land of Canaan is doled out, is found to be inside the area dominated by Judah. Eventually, Simeon is subsumed into Judah and passes into history. Levi and his tribe are not allotted any land in Canaan after it is conquered. They do get to be the line of priests, though, since Moses and his brother are from that tribe.

2. Benjamin is Jacob's second child of Rachel. Unfortunately, Rachel died during his birth. During the birth, Rachel named him Ben-Oni (son of my trouble). Jacob renamed him Benjamin (son of my right hand) in honor of Rachel, who was his most beloved. For a brief time, Benjamin was a pawn of Joseph's to get his father to come to Egypt. Benjamin had a small plot of land resulting from the distribution. It is centered around the city of Jerusalem.

3. Even though Joseph was a legitimate son of Jacob, he inherited no blessing from his father. Hey, who needs a dad's blessing when you are the pharaoh's right-hand man? Instead, Jacob blesses Joseph's two boys, Ephraim and Manasseh.

Thoughts About God

CHAPTER 12

Knowing God

It's simple.

You cannot.

You never will.

This is a foolish endeavor.

Stop with the hubris.

Walk away now.

The end.

CHAPTER 13

What Is in a Name?

The last chapter gave the best answer, but for those who want to learn a little more humility, let us pursue the question above. How can we know the god of the Hebrews and Christians? Is it possible to find him through religion or philosophy? Most people believe that to be the case—another chapter will delve deeper into this question. This chapter is but an overview that investigates the religious world as we know it today.

I will use the Hebrew *Adonai* in this chapter for the simple but real reason that the word denotes the exactness of what is being discussed. In Hebrew, that word means "the name." It will be used here to replace the tetragram (YHWH), which is the noun. To utter the holiness of the name by *human lips* is to profane the name, even when used with reverence. When reading the Torah or praying, the tetragram is said as Adonai, which means "lord," or, more accurately, "someone or something having power, authority, or influence." Our use of Adonai will honor that tradition, for this is spoken of in normal usage.

Again, as stated in the last chapter, you cannot know Adonai, for Adonai is wholly *other*. And for that, we will digest this idea and wonder at the hubris of those who have spent time and effort to know him. The notion of a human having the hubris to believe they, with their limited abilities to understand the infinite and ineffable Cosmic God, is laughable on its face. We need only look at the two testaments—Hebrew and Christian—to see two extremes. Each is radically different in the defining who the god they believe in is. Yet their god is the same. If you add in the Islamic god, who is the same god, you get a third option.

(Hmm, three gods in one. I have heard that song and dance somewhere.)

A warning to the reader: ride gently through the thoughts to come, for there will be doses of theology, metaphysics, logic, tradition, and the stubbornness of an old codger's mind when considering the following mumbo-jumbo. This discussion is broken into segments to keep track of how man has attempted to answer the question of knowing Adonai. We hear pastors doing their thing about getting up close and personal with the Cosmic Creator. Forests of trees became books that describe, in exceptionally fine detail, the length, and breadth and width of *who* he is and *what* he is. Scholars spend their lifetimes delving into putting shape and definition into this persona. As if that is possible! How can one parse what is related in either testament about knowing Adonai? Tradition says it is easy. How are the writings and thoughts and words prior to this moment to be put into a simple, distilled essence of understanding in our minds? Shall we take Maimonides's outlook, or perhaps Spinoza's rather caustic opinions? Do we prefer the Roman Catholic doctrinal spin or Martin Luther's point of view? Southern Baptist or Methodist? We even look at the Hebrew Bible or the Christian Bible. All these are well and good, but each one changes the landscape.

Naming Rights

Knowing the Creator God intimately is the desire and goal of people who profess belief. I understand this goal, and I admire the desire! This desire is even in the face of his words in Exodus, telling us in no uncertain terms that we will never be able to. In Genesis, in the oldest parts, the only name given for the Creator god was *Elohim*, which is not a personal name but a title.[1] Exodus gives us, in the Creator God's own words, his personal name: I AM. However, in our religious fervor and hubris, we do not accept what the very deity spoke. We refuse to accept his own answer to the question and work to pin Adonai down in an acceptable form and box with a neat bow on the top.

---

1   *Elohim* is the plural form of *Eloah*. Actually, it can be and often is used in the singular sense. The meaning is a descriptor of a god. When shortened to *El*, it most often refers to the head or chief god, but that is another story.

God said to Moses, "I Am *that*[2] I Am." And he said, "You must say this to the Israelites, 'I Am has sent me to you.'" —Exodus 3:14[3] (NET)

Rivers of ink have been poured out parsing what this word salad means. The exegesis of this statement varies, as it must. Are you ready for the answer to this conundrum? The Hebrew word structure of I Am THAT I Am gets complicated real fast. The three tenses: past, present, and future are used. Point in fact, the wording requires the three tenses to be used *simultaneously*. Each tense is interchangeable for each and every word! So which of these possible meanings is correct? The answer is easy-peasy; all are correct! It is too much for our minds to manage. Deal with the conundrum and sit humbly by in the unknowing because we are too limited to fully grasp the concept. Robert Alter, in his translation notes, says the Creator God "gave Moses more than he bargained for—not an identifying divine name ... but an ontological divine mystery of the most daunting character."[4]

My paraphrase: The Creator God told Moses, "Okay, buddy, you want my name, you got my name. You do not know what it means because it is too complicated and otherworldly to understand, but here you go. Oh, and when you tell my people, you will tell them exactly what I said to you."

We in the western world figured this was a really good verbal sleight-of-hand (voice?) magic trick. We are confident the expert scholars will work it out and have the trick understood in no time. But 2,500 years later, they are still working on it. Heh! Early Hebrew people and writers, in their humility, got the import of what was being said. The Creator God's name is *the concept of being or existence*. Does that make sense? An example of this is to imagine the number four. Hold out your hand and imagine that concept in your hand. Not something that adds up to four, but the *concept of the number four*.

What does it look like? How does it feel? Does it smell, and what color is it? What is its reality? We know beyond a doubt the number four is something real, yet it has no place in existence. That is what the Creator God is telling Moses, yet on an infinitely larger scale. The Hebrew writers got that and

2   The Hebrew word represented here can be translated as "that," "who," "which," and "what."

3   The Septuagint translation reads, "And God spoke to Moses, saying, I am THE BEING; and he said, Thus shall ye say to the children of Israel, THE BEING has sent me to you."

4   Robert Alter, 2018, *The Hebrew Bible: A Translation with Commentary*, W. W. Norton & Company.

created the tetragram YHWH. Their god *is*, but he is unexplainable in our world's words or concepts. Therefore, they refuse to speak the name of their god, or even spell it. *Adonai* is the word they use. Again, *Adonai* means "the name," which provides the best amount of respect and humility due to the Cosmic Creator God.

Philosophy

Let us look at this philosophically now. Philosophers are the ace in the hole for figuring this stuff out. Why are they our ace? Because they are the professionals of thinking and reasoning. Finding and filling logic holes in an argument is their bread and butter, so they tell us. The best thinkers of any age have been stumped for a straightforward answer to the dilemma of Adonai's name. Even getting the proper question that allows for an answer is unclear. When Jesus did his ascending-into-the-heavens thing, philosophers and theologians worked on what *happened* and *the real reason it happened*. That was easy compared to Adonai's name.[5]

Early on, differing viewpoints regarding these areas of thought sprang into being. Of course they differed. After several hundred years of saying bad things about the other side (and several slap fights among learned men), the winning belief system claimed the right to say what was orthodox. The others, the heretics, were put down—often into graves. From that point on, the orthodox system became the de facto way to believe. Orthodoxy even required that the proper way to believe was to listen and adhere to their authority on the Scriptures and their rules and dictates for living. This lasts even to this day.

Christianity

I will profess ignorance of the great thinkers of Islam, much to my chagrin. The same problem arises, however, with the noted thinkers of the other two Creator-God systems of belief, so there is that. Our western culture has been steeped in the notion that only scholars and religious leaders are trained to delve into such topics. And we let them. Where does this get us, Joe or

---

5   And no, Jesus ascending into heaven is disputed to this day. Did it really happen? Sure, why not?

Jane Pewsitter, on our journey to know Adonai? I often listen to a Sunday morning radio program with a preacher who plays fast and loose with Scripture, pulling verses out of context to prove whatever point he is making. He also says that if his listeners do not get what he is speaking about, they "need to find a well-qualified pastor" to help them understand what he is preaching. The radio preacher says that phrase more than once during his weekly rant. Why depend on a "well-qualified pastor" when we have the same set of Scriptures as the radio preacher?

I can walk and chew bubblegum at the same time without tripping. I am also able to read and understand weighty topics. Internet access is open on my other screen as I type these words. Articles on archaeology are readily available for finding tasty and pertinent information. Historical books are available. My bookshelves are crammed with good critical works by learned men. So why must I only listen to and follow the company line? I will bet most western Christians will say they know what they believe but do not know anything other than what has been preached at them. They have never gone out on the skinny branches to discover their truth.

Christianity proudly claims former writers and thinkers whose names are somewhat familiar and who we faintly know from history. Today, they are ciphers because we do not use their words or even their thinking anymore. Here is a short list of philosophers and scholars of the Early Christian era: Ignatius, Clement, Justin Martyr, Irenaeus, Origen, Tertullian, and Augustine. I am sure you recognize at least some of the names. Can you speak to their beliefs and how/if they are still reflected in our doctrines today? I am confident your "well-qualified pastor" cannot either. This is chiefly due to what is known today as progressive theology.[6]

These are the very philosophers who created the belief system for what is called Christianity. We do not read them anymore, much to our detriment, because we get new tomes of pseudo-philosophy/theology from authors every day that are on the New York Times best sellers list. When did you

---

6   Progressive theology has morphed into progressive Christianity. Either one is an insidious and backhanded way to finagle today's social topics into all that is biblical. We are to ignore what was meant by the writer and insert whatever social construct that is being highlighted today. The original writers did not have us as the intended audience and we, in our hubris, hurt the power of their message.

last hear of these past successful thinkers in a sermon or see one's name in the newest screed published yesterday? Saint Augustine, who wrote in the fourth century CE, is the father of our Christian belief system. His synthesis of the older writers makes his work so impressive and foundational. He was the person who completed the notion of original sin. Take that primary idea out of the Christian doctrine and see how quickly you get burned at the stake![7]

What is so impressive is that these past master philosophers were making it up as they went. Christianity was sparkling new, right off the showroom floor. (It even had that New Testament smell!) They had no handbook to explain the rules of the game. These philosophers used the Hebrew testament, the Gospels, and St. Paul's missives to work with. Other writings with other Christian philosophies were available to them, but those writings became banned because of heresies—even though the writers were respected scholarly peers. Marcion and Montanus were of this heretical ilk: influential, but with nonorthodox results. After 325 CE, the leaders were able to straighten things out when the Roman group of Christ-followers got permission to be the state religion. Of course, the first thing they did was remove the heretical beliefs—and the heretics.

Judaism

We turn to the Jewish belief system. Their writings have been around since the seventh century BCE, with writings still being put to paper later in the inter-testament period before Jesus of Nazareth's birth. During that time, the Hebrew belief system and its practices took several severe hits to its psyche. The final blow occurred when the temple was destroyed in 70 CE, and the ruins of that belief system wandered for centuries. The twelfth century CE brought forth a man, a philosopher, who transformed Hebrew thought. His profound thinking gave a clearer understanding of who the Hebrews were and why. This man was Moses ben Maimonides (the Rambam). A preeminent astronomer and physician, he also wrote extensively on the Torah. He had his critics during his lifetime, but after his death, he became revered as one of the foremost Jewish philosophers ever. We will discuss his ideas in a later chapter.

---

7   Stake, not steak. You are the one who got to be barbecued.

I think of the hubris we Christians possess when we ignore the thoughts and insights of such men as those above, Jewish and Christian. As Agent J says in the movie *Men in Black*, "They are old and busted." The legacies of these inspired men are put into the dark recesses of our beliefs for they are old, and we dare to think that we of today are more capable of parsing the words of the Scriptures, or, again, as Agent J says, our insights are the "new hotness." I challenge each one of you to read Maimonides and not come away with a much better awareness of the Cosmic God than any hundred sermons or books you name. It is our fault, and our shame is great.

Science versus YHWH

Science helps us see how unable we are to explain the Cosmic Creator God. Imagine the thought that if the Cosmic Creator God had a face, his smile right now is from ear to ear, and he is saying, "Bring it on! I want you to know more!" We will never know the Cosmic Creator God. But I see his essence, his being, all around. I am comfortable in the unknowing. How exciting to see what our scientific world will offer us tomorrow. The more we learn about the attributes of the Cosmic God, the more I realize I know less than when I started, which is what he was getting at with his statement to Moses, "I Am that which I Am."

The Cosmic God is not afraid of us. He has no fear of our learning about what life and earth and the cosmos is about. The Creator God does not worry when we question proof of his existence. *His existence IS*. The Cosmic Creator God does not need a defensive action to silly questions. From what we read in both testaments, Adonai's only request is that we honor him above all. Science has enriched us. Since Galileo pointed his telescope toward the night sky, our understanding of how the distant, gigantic galaxies— the cosmos—came to be is astounding. What is even more astounding is that they are made of the same subatomic particles that make you and me. Knowing we are composed of the same stuff created from long-dead stars strains my mind. Have you ever thought that every cell in your body is far more complicated than your cell phone or one of Elon Musk's starships? Science is not our enemy. Every discovery by science tells us more and more that we cannot fathom the Creator. But Adonai desires us to learn more.

The writers of either testament did not put science into either portion of Scripture. Genesis 1 is not, and never has been, about science. Stop with the parsing of the chronologies. They changed as needed to illuminate a storyline. Quit pitting Charles Darwin against that idiot James Ussher. Please do not require science to conform to the Scriptures. Please do not require the Scriptures to conform to science. Remember, the Cosmic Creator God is not corporeal. Science only deals in the world that can be measured. The Cosmic Creator God, Adonai, cannot be measured, for he is outside of creation. Do you see the misunderstanding now?

Such silly demands from both sides are akin to requiring a baseball game to be judged under the rules of football, or worse yet, tiddly-winks. What a profane idea! To deride religion from a scientific viewpoint or science from a religious stance makes fools of both sides. Adonai desires us to know everything that makes our world work and to benefit from that knowledge. Science has a rule that requires knowledge to be built around the consideration that it can (if possible) be disproved. There is a story describing when Einstein was shown a German newspaper that claimed, "One hundred German physicists claim Einstein's theory of relativity is wrong." Einstein's reply was supposedly, "If I were wrong, it would only take one." Religion gives an opinion and declares it to be the truth, and nevermore shall it be questioned. Ouch!

Tradition

Now we shall turn to tradition. Imagine Tevye singing "Tradition!" from the movie *Fiddler on the Roof.* The upshot of this song is the heartache of keeping a society running as it always had while the world around it changes. My children will attest to my manifold rants about the traditions of the church. The rant goes something like this: "What a stupid rule. Why must we blindly follow the acts and thoughts of our betters?" We must not ask questions that lead to disbelief, apostasy, or heresy. How we shall live is dictated from on high, from the past. I am sure when my children read this section, their eyes will roll, just as they did when they were younger!

The truth is, this refrain that comes from on high in ecumenical circles is, "Trust us, we know what is best for you." Even more, in the words of the philosopher of the 1930s, Chico Marx, "Who are you going to trust, me or your lying eyes?" How many of us regular people have done the work ourselves to gain any understanding of knowing the Yahweh Elohim of the testaments? Are we sheep, so beholden to tradition that we see no other way than to obey only that which has been presented to us?

What do our Christian betters teach us about knowing Adonai? We have the Apostles' Creed. The Catholic church has its pope. Protestant churches use their own separate book of rules, their discipline, doctrine, or dogma. Since 1978, we have even had sixteen rules regarding expectations we are to hold regarding the Scriptures, which you must agree to.[8] Are these rule-makers and rulebooks logical and biblically based? More importantly, are these rules about knowing Adonai better? Prayer, Christian fellowship, worship, and walking in the Spirit will do the trick, we are told. The problem is those tasks are only about keeping your membership in your local Jesus club. But nothing in these regulations will bring an understanding of Adonai. I was once castigated for not raising my hands in praise to Adonai properly.[9] Such rules! We Christians pity the poor, foolish Jews for their 613 laws of obedience. At least they have their guidelines written, so everybody knows the proper game plan. Do a Google search for Christian rules and laws. You will find no fewer than eight hundred commands. These rules and laws are acceptable—they are not officially official, but they are written in the Christian testament, just as the 613 Jewish laws are found in the Tanakh. Going to an evangelical church service today is fraught with the potential for faux pas. Icky.

Recalibration

I refuse to let this become a polemic against the churches of today. There is much good in Christianity that offers hope for people who are missing something in their life. Churches would blossom if the focus was placed on what Jesus, not St. Paul, said. The mission statement for Jews is found below.

---

8   I refer to the Chicago Statement on Biblical Inerrancy (1978). Following in 1982 came the Chicago Statement on Biblical Hermeneutics. In 1986, we were saddled with the Chicago Statement on Biblical Application.

9   I did not realize how one's hands were positioned meant anything. No, this concept is not biblical. I punch the sky when my team makes a touchdown, and no one in the stadium cares how that punch looks. If church people are grading hand positions during a service, they need to rethink their mindset.

This is what Jesus said to be the most important command. They say Moses' words twice a day. Jesus repeated those words. I have begun this practice and offer it to you now.

> Jesus answered, "The most important command is this: *'Listen, people of Israel! The Lord our God, he is the only Lord. Love the Lord your God. Love him with all your heart, all your soul, all your mind, and all your strength.'"* — Mark 12:29–30 (IBC)

I have put Moses' words in italics, but it is Jesus speaking. This is the Shema, taken from Deuteronomy 6:4–5.[10] It is the fundamental idea from which all else springs from in the Hebraic belief system. All ideas, rules, and observances *must conform to* and *confirm* this statement, or else they are cast aside. We Christians have that from our founder's (Jesus') mouth, as seen above, yet we glibly (or in one of my more famous rants, stupidly) pass it over for the Apostles' Creed.

Evangelicals sit weekly and meekly in our pews or comfy chairs while pretty music, smoke, and lights entertain us and some "well-qualified" pastor aims some words at our heads. We never open our Bibles to confirm or deny what is said or sung. We are sheep. It is easier that way. All that allows us to coast along during the rest of the week, knowing we did exactly as we have been told is our religious duty. Evangelicals ought to be ashamed and feel bad for our inactivity. My father, may he rest in peace, was known for this statement: "Know what you believe." I, in the not-too-distant past, realized I did not know what I believed. Yet there is a verse that had nagged at me through my life:

> Do your best to present yourself to God as one approved, a workman who has no need to be ashamed, rightly handling the word of truth.
> —2 Timothy 2:15 (ESV)

I had done my best, I thought. I spewed the company line blindly. Despite not knowing what any of it meant. Scripture verses came easily to prove my (Protestant belief system) point. Something still nagged, something missing. I realized it when I argued the Calvinist versus Arminian doctrines, the battle

---

10   This refers back to Deuteronomy 6. This is the Hebrew transliteration: "All the heart of you, and in all the soul of you, and in all of utterly you."

of the ages, with a friend.[11] Thank goodness we both had incredibly wise counsel, which went like this: "He believes in the same god as you. You are positive you will go to heaven, as he is also assured. Does it matter the steps one takes if the road is pointed to the same ending?" Simple, distinct, easy to understand. It does not matter what large words and lengthy arguments surround doctrines. It really does not matter if there are doctrines. It is the endpoint that matters. And it is my responsibility, no one else's, to ensure my following to that endpoint.

Conclusion

"I do believe; help me overcome my unbelief!" (Mark 9:24). Do I know Adonai? No! However, I rest easy in the unknowing of who this Adonai is. For not knowing is part of the journey. I know what I know. As I learn more, I understand there is more to know! I accept my growing lack of knowledge. That is okay for now. The biggest takeaway for me is the ability to start asking the right questions. Questions that do not require a scientific answer. Answers that do not involve convoluted philosophical or theological corkscrew thinking.

All else will fall into place or not.

---

11   What is the Calvin versus Arminius argument about? If you know, you know. If you do not, thank the good Lord and keep reading.

CHAPTER 14

Maimonides Steps to the Plate

Christianity works hard to one-up other religions, with special emphasis aimed at its older brother. The god of Christians' worship is described in huge and glorious terms, filling one with awe and wonder. Mighty hymns are written, and grand cathedrals are raised. They are there to give note to their god's utter majesty. Vast armies have striven to destroy those other puny religions on the back of their glorious god. People from all walks of life have given their lives to attain the transcendence of a glimpse of the Christian god's majesty. How many weighty tomes and treatises have arisen in the attempt to uncover a glimpse of the god's greatness? They claim power and might and glory and dominion over all for the Christian god.

And yet they call him by his nickname. And not just call him by his nickname but mock their older religious brother for keeping the respect their god is due. Judaism gives their god the respect due to the point that they will not even say the Cosmic Creator God's name, using only a tetragram to spell it out. Adding to that, they even use a word to indicate they are referring to the tetragram. Now that, my friend, is respect, honor, and humility. And a good reason to stop and think for a moment. I have spent my life understanding how a person can know such a god who, from the beginning, was outside the entire process of creation. The more I heard of who God was, the more I cringed. Each of the sermons and religious writings I encountered kept defining the Cosmic Creator God down into a nice, neat pigeonhole. A box. That box has a pretty bow tie on it, however, which is supposed to make it all well and good. What is a poor preacher's kid to do with all of this? Every portrayal boxed my god into a smaller and smaller prison. Such an oxymoron; God is totally unknowable, yet the list of God's beingness grew longer and longer to the point I could not see him any differently than a standard typical human hero. Without a cape, of course (at Edna's insistence).

Christian Definition of Adonai

Too often we hear the phrase "God is (*insert quality here*)." That does not work for me. Too much human, not enough divine. Too often the "insert quality here" is spoken as the truth—foundational, not to be examined, and, dare I say it, inerrant and infallible. Far too often, the quality is not even biblical! Why do we western minds demand to understand something fully when we know it is out of our capability? Defining something means putting boundaries around that something. When you "know" something, you are able to put limits on its space, time, and function. And yet, with our very same mouths and words, we insist our god cannot be described or limited. Our attempts to do so merely make the Cosmic God less and puts us on a higher level than we should be. Over time, we keep shrinking the Christian god into smaller and smaller boxes, all the while smiling and patting ourselves on the back.

We are speaking of the Cosmic Creator God. The entity who was there before *there* was a *there* to be there! Sit with that thought a moment. Christian scholars use the term for the creation events of Genesis 1 as *ex nihilo*, which is Latin for "from nothing." The term *creation ex nihilo* refers to the Cosmic God creating everything from nothing. Um, yes, there definitely was something, maybe. If there was nothing, where and what was the Cosmic God? Was he nothing or something? If he were nothing, then he was part of the creation event. If he were something, when there was nothing, how in the entire world of religion, philosophy, and myth could he be explained?

Perhaps an analogy would help. We all know of the Big Bang theory. We know about cosmic background radiation, the inflation period, and what happened in the first trillionth of a second. Also, we know how freaking hot everything was for hundreds of thousands of years, which even kept atoms from forming. Ok, fine. But what happened in the first trillionth of a second *before* the big was banged? We do not know or have any real clue of how to figure that problem out. I know of theorists who have invented many wonderful conjectures, but we have absolutely *no* way to resolve this issue. We have the same conundrum with defining the Cosmic Creator God. Science is flummoxed about this. Western theology does not provide any answers, for there is no reason to consider such things. Theology studies interactions with people and their god. Science can only answer material clues. If something has form, function, and a location, science is your go-to. There is, however, one theory I hold to be the best possible example of what happened prior to creation (or the Big Bang).

For that, I turn to thinkers of the fantastic—the realm of science fiction. Here is the last bastion of thinking and dreaming outside of the box, of using our minds as the Cosmic Creator God intended, to ply the boundaries of the real and unknown. Isaac Asimov wrote a brief treatise on this subject in 1956, and I invite you to read "The Last Question." Here is a most satisfying but humbling story that invites us to consider questions that elude orthodox thinking. We have the Big Bang theory, and we have the creation story. We have no answer to what went on before these two momentous events. The Judeo-Christian beliefs have a Cosmic Creator, a something, hanging around in the nothingness. Again, get your mind around *how there can be something when there is nothing.* Science says that is impossible, and I believe it. Western religion says otherwise, and I have no problem with this either.

We humans—Albert Einstein and Elon Musk included—are capable of a mental brilliance that astonishes me. We see the magnificence of SpaceX's reusable rockets and do not have a problem wrapping our minds around how our forebears figured out how to harness fire. Do you know how many societies never understood the wheel? Columbus was a jerk in so many ways, but his belief and his actions made the world so much larger and stranger. We are the beneficiaries of his insane inspiration! The stirrup was invented early in China and the Mongols "exported" it to Europe in the Middle Ages. The transistor was invented in 1947. It has transformed our world in countless ways. I assure you, if you search for science fiction inventions written about in the 1950s and 1960s, some fanciful ideas became reality. What wonders you will find: mobile phones, the moon landing, personal digital assistants, artificial intelligence, credit cards, and the e-reader you are possibly using to read this.

And yet, our conceptualization of a Cosmic Creator God squashes us down instantly, rightly showing our hubris. Of course, our ego will not allow us to quit, so we continue to play philosophical and theological games to make ourselves look smarter than we know we are. Silly us! The Hebrew people have enough humility to understand the problem with such thinking. Hence, the refusal to say the Cosmic Creator's name and never write it, except in code. We western Christians use happy music and smoke and colored lights to delight our feelings in worship while the Hebrew people use their minds and hearts.

Humility is not a well-respected aspect of American life, despite what is preached. We find evidence of this from even only a brief time ago—for example, the refusal to admit defeat even when it is obvious to everyone else that we are outnumbered and outgunned. During World War II, Brigadier General Anthony McAuliffe's 101st armored division was surrounded by the Germans. The Germans demanded complete surrender, or the Americans would be annihilated. Vastly outnumbered, low on supplies and in the freezing cold, McAuliffe's response to the Germans comprised of one word: "Nuts!" And the 101st defeated the opposition quite handily.

Washington's Army of the Republic was not superior to the British, yet here we are, 250 years later, a nation. The winter at Valley Forge was devastating. Our celebrated battle at Bunker Hill in Boston was a horrible defeat for the colonials. America did not really win the Revolutionary War. We merely outlasted Britain, and they left. We were completely outnumbered and outgunned and outmaneuvered in the World War II Battle of Midway but beat the Japanese and turned the tide in the Pacific. Martin Luther King Jr. demanded peaceful protests against the Deep South's governance and won. Shall we go on?

Western religion has no humility toward its Creator God. Because it has worked so far, westerners (and I include Europe) regurgitate the traditional mores and values from long ago. Protestant and Catholic practices and religious history have, however, worked to ensure one should not step out of bounds. These bounds include how we are to view the god of our religion as told by an authority. Our self-pride tells us we can figure God out. This is much like building our own Tower of Babel. That thought, my friends, leaves me cold.

Of what does our tower comprise? Let us start with inerrancy, infallibility, tradition, authority, and inspiration of the Bible. The Apostles' Creed, Nicene Creed, worship of the Scriptures, and the sinner's prayer are some longer-winded laws that must be conformed to and never questioned by evangelicals. Since Constantine, monies have been extracted from followers for soaring and inspiring edifices instead of helping and ministering to the widows and orphans, even though the latter is what Jesus of Nazareth insisted upon.

Glittering generalities from an authority figure occurred then and today, instead of the hard, persistent work required to understand the Scriptures. Jesus himself ministered to those truly in need. Differing opinions are not allowed in discussions. All must conform. And in our hubris, we still call the Cosmic Creator casually by his nickname. Let us get back to the Cosmic Creator and see if we can find another way to see him in all his glory. If we are willing, let us allow ourselves to remove our ego and raise our humility in this exercise. This next part will be rather rough for some, as it will disrupt what has always been in one's mind and way of thinking. I am not going out on a heretical limb—far from it. What will happen is thinking at a different level, to see if we can glean an insight into why using a tetragram for the Cosmic Creator's name is good for the Hebrew religion and good for us. Ready?

Negative Theology

These three statements are all true:

1. *I believe in God, but I do not believe he exists.*

2. *God is incapable of being good.*

3. *God is not omnipresent.*

Do I have your hackles up yet? Good. This is a sampling of apophatic theology, also known as *via negativa* or *via negationis*. Originally conceived in the late fifth and early sixth century CE by the Christian Neoplatonist Pseudo-Dionysius, it was heavily worked over by Moses Maimonides (the Rambam) in the twelfth century. He dubbed it negative theology (apophasis). Maimonides's thesis is that we are able to know the Cosmic Creator only in the negative.

Here we have a question that directs us from the path we took before, allowing us to consider our precepts from another angle. We are then able to ponder anew, if we are not too invested in the traditional way of thinking. What might one find by considering something from other points of view? Until Maimonides, the orthodox logic structure was to define the god by implying his essence, which therefore proves his existence. Maimonides, instead, starts with defining the world and works to logically imply the existence of God. I will bet you never heard this from any preacher! Maimonides took several hundred pages to explain this concept. I will attempt to simplify his work into a few paragraphs. My hope is to do his work justice because this exercise is important for what will follow.

Let us consider our astral friend, the sun. Our sun is a material object; it occupies a specific place in time and location. We know what it is and where it is located at any moment in time. (I know it is present because it is mighty hot here in Tucson right now.) Because we know the sun is present and where it is, we also know it is not infinite. We have proof of this from Albert Einstein's theory of relativity, $E=mc^2$. For our purposes, this formula requires that if one has infinite energy, it cannot be anything material. Therefore, the sun is finite, and it can only contain a finite amount of power of its being.[1] However, the sun and all heavenly bodies move through space freely, which implies an infinite amount of power, yet we know infinity cannot be present because they are material—they are made of molecules and atoms.

---

[1]   According to Dr. Louis Barbier, a cosmic ray astrophysicist with NASA, the sun creates "roughly 5 × 1023 horsepower, or what can be called 3.8 × 1033 ergs per second." What does that mean? Barbier answered that question too: "It is enough energy to melt a bridge of ice two miles wide, one mile thick, and extending the entire way from the earth to the sun in one second." (Understand Solar, n.d., "How Much Energy Does the Sun Produce?" https://understandsolar.com/how-much-energy-does-the-sun-produce/#:~:text=But%2C%20how%20much%20energy%20does,x%201033%20ergs%20per%20second.%E2%80%9D.)

Elegantly explained by both Rambam and Einstein, infinite power cannot be contained in a finite space: it must therefore be noncorporeal. If it is noncorporeal, it is not subject to division or change. Everything we know of today is composed of something. Science calls this composition *mass*. We see this in Einstein's equation, which is what the *m* stands for. If something has mass, it had to be created—something made it. Maimonides believes this gives us grounds for being able to say *that Yahweh is* but does not allow us to say *what Yahweh is*. We have absolutely no way to compare the Cosmic Creator God to anything, I repeat, *anything* else.

> There is no oneness at all except in believing that there is one simple essence in which there is no complexity or multiplicity of notions, but one notion only; so that from whatever angle you regard it and from whatever point of view you consider it, you will find that it is one, not divided in any way and by any cause into two notions.[2]

Here is where it gets really fun. By making the statement, "God is (*insert attribute here*)," you are creating a composite of two things. The composite consists of the word *is* and *the attribute*. If Yahweh were a composite of the two, something would have had to bring them together and keep them together. There would have to be a cause prior to the Cosmic God. (Something before the something that was before the nothing, as stated above). Go back to the three statements above and consider them from this apophasis (negative) way of thinking:

1. *I believe in God, but I do not believe he exists.* How can something without mass but with infinite power exist on any imaginable plane? Yet there is something inside us that compels a belief in some "higher power." "Higher power" infers the meaning is outside our realm of understanding that influences us. We see proof of this in the ancient past as well as today.

2. *God is incapable of being good.* Good is an ephemeral idea. One cannot reach out and grasp, touch, or smell "good." We, however, understand the concept of good—but only compared to something, and that other something is termed "bad." Science has no tangible

---

2   Maimonides, Moses, trans. M. Friedlander, 1910, *The Guide for the Perplexed*, George Routledge & Sons LTD.

way to present temperature unto itself. The only effective way for temperature to be measured is by comparing a level of heat to another level of heat. Such is why God cannot be good. What is an infinite, non-material subject to be compared to? If the god was good, there would have to be a badness somewhere. And from this, we find the dregs of the idea of Satan and his minions.

3. *God is not omnipresent.*[3] I like this example. If God is everywhere, he must be somewhere, which implies a physical embodiment of something. Yet we now know that, with infinite power, there cannot be any materialness attached to that power. Ergo, the Cosmic Creator God is incapable of being omnipresent. Yet we also know from Yahweh's own words of his promise never to leave us alone. So there is that!

4. *God is not all powerful.*[4] I will add one last apophasis, for it highlights the power of negative thinking. Even with everything considered above, this might not be obvious. The standard argument goes as such: If our god is all powerful, he will be able to create an object he cannot move. Yet if he could not move such an object, he would not be all powerful. What a delightful conundrum that jars our normal way of thinking! But do you see the error? The question is illogical. This question phrased differently looks like this: Can the god make a triangle with only one side? Other than in professional wrestling, the god cannot make a squared circle. The god, by his nature, can do anything that is possible—according to his nature. Back to the question, to make an impossibly large stone, that stone would have to take up all of space. (Einstein says this, along with St. Augustine and Maimonides.) Where would God be moving it to, if all space was taken up by the rock? This argument is silly and incoherent on its face. Rephrase the question into a sophism.[5] Is God capable of being incapable? This assumes that the nature of omnipotence allows for a power to compromise itself and

---

3　Omnipresence is the state of being everywhere at once (or seeming to be everywhere at once).

4　Omnipotence is having unlimited or universal power, authority, or force; all-powerful.

5　Sophism is a subtly deceptive reasoning or argumentation.

its nature. Putting "God can" before a nonsensical statement does not suddenly make the statement sensible.

Humans have a taxonomy that tells us we are part of the animal kingdom. We are made up in part by breathing air, having a backbone, and having cells with a nucleus. This structure is, of course, done when comparing us to other parts of the animal kingdom. Even in the first creation story, there is a delimiting between the fish, birds, air-breathing animals, and humanity. Therefore, according to Maimonides, we had a causal start. Something brought all these parts together and made us what we are today. One cannot say that about the Cosmic God. I do not even know what it means to say *god was before anything*. He is beyond human experience or imagination. Even using the pronoun *he* in this discourse causes upset because it assumes something that is not!

Now, if you have been reading along and hopefully following this line of reasoning, you see problems. Maimonides does state that both negative (apophatic) and positive (cataphatic) statements of God are problematic in their adding complexity. God is neither *and* nor *not*.

> Know that when you make an affirmation ascribing another thing to Him, you become more remote from Him in two respects: one of them is that everything You affirm is a perfection only with reference to us, And the other is that He does not possess a thing other than His essence.[6]

Conclusion

And here is the nut of the thinking. We, in our hubris, think we can corral the Cosmic Creator God into something that suits our inclinations. We take our human knowledge, and, with our ego, imagine we know enough to think we're on the level to be on a first-name basis with the Cosmic Creator God. Rodney Dangerfield always griped about not getting respect. We evangelicals give our Creator even less respect.

Citing Psalm 65, Maimonides concludes that the highest form of praise we offer Yahweh is silence about who he is. Rather, we should speak of

---

6   Maimonides, *The Guide for the Perplexed.*

the tangible benefits we see about us. That is why I understand why those of the Jewish religion act in the manner they do when not speaking their god's name. They are giving proper respect to the Cosmic Creator God, with silence and reverence and great humility. Would that the Christian churches might shut up and be humble before the Creator God.

Other (Mostly) Genesis Thoughts

CHAPTER 15

Understanding Translations

Þu fæder ure ðe eart on heofonum.
Sy þin nama gehalgod.
ecume þin rice.
i þin willa swa on heaofonum
ond eac on eorðan.
Syle us todæg urne dæghwomlican half
ond forgif us ure giltas.
Swa swa we forgifað þam þe wið us agiltað
ond ne læt þu na us on costnunge.
Ac alys us fram yfele.
Si hit swa.

I thought I would start off with the most beloved prayer in the Christian Bible. Jesus himself taught it to his disciples and followers, and if you have spent any time around a church, you've memorized it. It is, of course, the Lord's Prayer, but you knew that, didn't you?

Wait, what do you mean you didn't recognize it? It's in English. Well, Old English. This is the way our language was written and spoken around 1000 CE. It is descended from ancient Germanic, which includes southern Scandinavia and most northern parts of Germany. We also know Old English as Anglo-Saxon, named for the two tribes that invaded and settled in England in the fifth century CE. A mere thousand years later, and we cannot read or understand this gibberish.

All this trivia is nice to know, but what does any of it have to do with understanding the Bible and what is in it? Well, everything. And that is the discussion for this chapter. I bring this example from our past to help us more clearly understand the difficulties of reading and attaining meaning from the Bible's works from ages past. This example from our not-too-distant past will do well for how we will process translations of the inspired words of both testaments. Here is the literal (transliteration) breakdown of the above prayer:

Our Father, thou that art in heavens,
Be thy name hallowed.
To come thy kingdom.
Become thy will in earth so as in heavens.
Give to us today our day only loaf.
And forgive to us our guilts,
So as we forgive to our guilting ones.
And not lead thou us into temptation.
But release us from evil.
Be it so.

This is an excellent example of what a translator has to contend with—strange letters we no longer use, the odd syntax of the sentences, and, more importantly, how the vernacular of its specific time denotes meaning. By that last note, look at the original prayer. Do you notice the "swa swa"? *Swa*, at that time, meant "as." This we see from the transliteration. However, when used twice, it connotes a stronger idea. Here, we see it being used to denote a thought with the power of using "just as," or to use a more contemporary term, "exactly as." An example in today's language is someone who stands at the edge of the Grand Canyon for the first time. They stand at the edge, looking out at the expanse, attempting to describe the sight. On first thought, that viewer marvels, "That is big." But that is not strong enough, so they try again: "That is really big." Still, there is something missing in that statement. A third attempt evinces the right emotion: "That is really, *really* big!" That is the same concept as what that "swa swa" is doing.

On another tidbit, I like the ending of the translation: *Be it so/So be it*. We usually end our theological meanderings with an *amen*,[1] which is the same idea. Our constant use of *amen* has ground the edges of that word's impact to the point where we of today do not get the import. We can see changes happening in today's vernacular. For example, as discussed in a previous chapter, the word *decimate* is evolving from its original Latin meaning of killing one tenth of a regiment to inflicting great damage or the destruction of something. I am sure, soon enough, the old, proper meaning will have disappeared forever.

My prayer is that this book will be silly. I most certainly will be unhappy if my writing is nice. *Silly* originally meant "worthy" or "blessed," and *nice* was originally "foolish" or "simple."

Words, over time, can take on opposite meanings, often simultaneously. When seeding a lawn, you are adding something. Seeding a watermelon requires removing parts. Trimming a tree obviously needs some contextual understanding of the situation. Context helps with the word *fast*. Do you

---

1   *Amen* is an expression used at the end of prayers, meaning "so be it." At the end of a creed, it is a solemn asseveration of belief. When it introduces a declaration, it is equivalent to "truly, verily," as was often used by Jesus when offering a parable.

mean secured in place, or moving quickly? If you are *sanctioning* an action or person, are you permitting or prohibiting that action or person? Words in English, as well as other languages, have more than one definition. The word *run* has 645 different, and often divergent, meanings. The word *go* gets second place with 430. *Take, stand, set, turn, fall,* and *strike* have more than two hundred definitions each. Context will tell which meaning should be taken. Who could have realized a little three-letter word like run could be one of the most complicated words in the English language! English is a language that informs us of the context by other words in the sentence. Other languages spoken today have prefixes and suffixes on the word to do the work, making sentence structure shorter, and in some cases, more coherent.

The sounds of our twenty-six letters have changed a lot. English vowels used to sound the same as the Romance languages, but over the course of three hundred years during the Great Vowel Shift, the sounds changed to be what they are today.[2] Reread the Lord's Prayer above and vocalize the vowels as a Spanish or French speaker would today. Also, our letter *C* has changed dramatically. Remember, if you will, in Rome during Jesus' time, the letter *C* sounded like our *K* today. Over time, it softened into the *S* sound. Later still, it changed to the *CH* sound in Romance languages. The last iteration in its move about the sounding board brought us to the *SH* sound. All the while, it kept its prior sounds but added another vocalization. What an attention hound that *C* is![3] These changes are how linguists tell the age of words that contain the letter *C*. How it is pronounced will give its given place in history. The word for the imperial leader of Germany before the mustachioed man taking over the country was Kaiser. The pronunciation of *Kaiser* is the same as what the first *Caesar* of Rome was called. And the meaning of *Kaiser* is the same as the first Roman emperor. What hubris that was, to compare the leader of a tiny country to an ancient leader of a vast empire!

Few letter sounds have stayed the same. Letters were added and subtracted as needed by the usage of the people. Sounds have also been added or

---

2   The Great Vowel Shift occurred mainly between the fifteenth and eighteenth centuries. Prior to the shift, English vowels were pronounced as the Romance languages do today (ah, eh, ee, oh, ooh).

3   *Caesar-pronounced Kaiser* (early Roman), *circa* (late roman), *chief* (middle French), *chef* (late French)

displaced through time and location.[4] The Japanese were mocked in World War II for their inability to pronounce *L* and *R*. Simply put, these sounds were never used in their speech until they had to deal with pesky westerners. We English-users are unable to say the *X* sound at the start of a word, so we replaced its sound with the *Z* sound. With that in mind, we should not think poorly of the Japanese. Often, older languages have fewer words to denote meaning as compared to our current way of thought. And if a word appears that is not familiar, one needs to look at other sources to glean what is meant, although some words are never used elsewhere. *Hapax legomenon* is a Greek term that means "being said once." An exceptionally good example is from the flood narrative. We are told the craft being built was made of gopher wood. The word only occurs here in the Torah. What the tree described is uncertain. The Targum Onkelos[5] renders it "cedar." The Septuagint translates it as "squared" timber, and the Vulgate translation is "smoothed" timber. Modern commentators suppose some conifer suitable for shipbuilding must be meant. Yet there is no definite answer to this question. Here we have to take guesses and hope they suit the narrative. Scholars throw up their hands and eyes toward the sky, sigh, and do their best.

As seen above, colloquialisms have been in use since the earliest of times. Say "throwing the rock" or "a frozen rope" to a sports fan. They immediately know you are referring to football and baseball. Saying "9/11" does the same thing for Americans. In our present age, we have no problem understanding what those terms mean. Looking back into the past, however, the opposite is true. On the historical timeline, writing is rather new. Only in the last five thousand years has any putting-the-oral-tradition-into-permanent-written-form been used. The earliest forms of written communication are simple and raw. Subtlety was not really a thing. Simplicity—few words with a myriad of meanings or ideas—are principles in those works. Yet translators see the amazing use of puns and wordplay,[6] such that, frankly, it should embarrass writers of today (this author included). Sadly, those verbal antics do not translate well.

---

4   Kevin Stroud's podcast, *The History of English*, is a fun, well-documented journey through the entire life of the English language. Our language started at the same location and time as the languages we are considering in this book. I highly recommend a listen.

5   Targum Onkelos is considered the oldest Jewish Aramaic targum (translation).

6   In the first four chapters of Genesis alone are *adam* (humanity)/*adamah* (ground), *isha* (woman)/*ish* (man), *arummim* (naked)/*arum* (cunning), *qanah* (gotten)/*qanan* (Cain).

Archaeology has also been a great boon to understanding what is meant in our Bible. Vast troves of literature have been discovered by those who dig into the earth. One learns of life in Mesopotamia, Egypt, Anatolia, and societies before the Greeks dominated the historical scene. Each language had its own form of writing with pictures and scratches that denoted ideas. The Phoenician and Ugarit cultures started using an alphabet that was based on sounds instead of ideas. Linguists are able to compare languages, and by doing so, gain knowledge in detecting how differing cultures used different words to describe the same meaning. It is the work of genius to see the similarity of words to one another.

The Egyptians used pictures for words and concepts. Sometime in the early second millennium BCE, the Aegean cultures used an ideographic and syllabic alphabet known as Linear B. Ancient Mesopotamia had a lettering system that used chisel-shaped marks, which is known as Cuneiform. Ancient Hebrew used a prototype of our alphabet, but there were no written vowels. We have even located the language of the Minoan proto-palatial civilization from the second millennium BCE era known as Linear A. On their face, they are wildly dissimilar from anything. Linguists, after decades, are still attempting to decipher Linear A.

Inside these disparate language structures, noticeable changes can be seen. Changes to how a letter is written can be seen to evolve. Consider the first letter in the prayer at the beginning of this chapter. It looks like a lowercase *P* with the round part having drifted down. That letter, called "thorn," was common for millennia. We now use two letters, *TH*, to mimic its sound. Word endings were where the action of the sentence was hidden. Understanding them is a must for acquiring insight into what was written. Try learning Latin, and you will spend more time learning what the proper way is to begin and end the word than the actual root word. Today's English has rid us of most of these translation stumbling blocks, but it has required us to use additional words to offer the same idea. Biblical Criticism, the bane of fundamental evangelists everywhere, delves deeply into this science, and we are blessed with their findings—even though these discoveries trouble many and cause others to rethink centuries of tradition.

Consider what has been learned so far. Word meanings, sentence structures, and euphemisms change over time. Even letters change shape and can be lost or gained.[7] A scholar sees and notes these differences. They then seek outside sources to identify and date when those styles and forms were similar. Is the construction of the word or sentence consistent with the dating, and does it refer to what is going on in the world at that time? The scholar determines much from such questions with the resources available from the region and its neighbors. We must remember, however, the vast majority of all that goes on in those ages past was in oral form, which does not allow researchers to know when such thoughts originally occurred. Even though we have vast quantities of permanent records from those ancient of days, those quantities are relatively few compared to the times and places they represent.[8]

All this is rather generic for life lived millennia ago. I want us to get more personal. Look at the Lord's Prayer again. It is obvious our English has evolved over the centuries. Consider now a document from the mid-1700s. Our Declaration of Independence is a most excellent example. The mode of speech is most definitely not like our current tongue. Look at how letters are formed. Why does the letter *S* look like an *F* in places? Who writes in cursive anymore? Getting even closer to our day, consider Mickey Spillane's hard-nosed detective, Mike Hammer, and his antics. Those books were written just after World War II. Compare Mike Hammer to Craig Johnson's sheriff, Walt Longmire, published in the early 2000s. Both series are great reads, but Longmire is more familiar because the lingo fits into the world of today.

Language develops as life's circumstances evolve. Seen from above, one can learn much from observing this change. This gives us the ability to see if and how sixty-six books written over fifteen hundred years came to be as we know them. The works found in the Bible as a whole are in the original Hebrew, Aramaic, and Greek. These three languages have gone through numerous evolutions that must be considered when reading the works. Syntax, letters, and context must be accounted for to understand what the writers intended, for that is the ultimate job of a translator. To complicate

---

7   English has gained several letters recently. J, 1640; V, 1400s; W,1700; X, 1400s.

8   At last count, there are approximately 52,000 different Bible-related texts for study.

matters even more, the *Sitz im Leben*[9] must be considered. Next, we will investigate the joys of translating—the thrills and chills of putting someone else's intentions into our eyes and ears.

Missing Letters

The Hebrew language did much the same with their speech and alphabet. Hebrews played much the same linguistic game over history. Originally, there were no vowels in the Hebrew language—at least, not until Aaron ben Moses ben Asher put vowel markings into the Masoretic text in the tenth century CE. Let us play a little game. Imagine English words without the vowels. *Rn* is an easy word to begin with. Does the writer mean run, ran, earn, or even urn? The meaning of the sentence will change with each. How about *thn*. We could have then or than, thin or thine, or perhaps even Ethan. *Spk* gets harder for us. Speak, spoke, spook, and spike are candidates. See how this problem can cause concern and confusion for a reader centuries later to get the gist of what is being said? One other game that is played within these early languages is the direction of flow. We English read from left to right. Hebrew is from right to left. Other languages can go either way. Several Asian languages go from top to bottom. Such reading markers as paragraphs and even spaces between words were not a thing for millennia.[10] The lack of paragraphs and spacing was common even in Paul's time when writing the New Testament! And don't forget about chapters and verses.[11]

The books of the Bible were meant to be read just as Hemingway's works were to be read: start to finish. Chapter and verse-imposed divisions, which are helpful to scholars and preachers, should be banned from any holy book. They are pernicious and harmful, for they allow preachers to dissect and use ideas that, when taken out of context, connote different meanings that the original writer did not intend. This is the reason why the selections listed in this book have no verse markings.

Fortunately, we have a Batman looking over this ancient-language Gotham.

---

9   Setting in life.

10   Paragraphs: Sixteenth century CE. Spaces: Formalized by Irish monks in the seventh century CE.

11   Chaptering started in the thirteenth century. Verses in the sixteenth century. Even these separation markers have evolved. Hebrew and Christian works differ in their separation concepts.

Archeo-linguists are scholars who study the evolution of ancient languages. We do not see such in our modern translations since we are living and breathing users of what is current, but scholars who do read Hebrew, Aramaic, and Greek comprehend things like flow direction, lack of spaces and vowels, and colloquialisms that influence what a word means. These language archaeologists are familiar with extrabiblical tongues, as they must be. These outside sources allow understanding, for there is no spoken or written vocabulary in the Bible that is not influenced by the outside world.

People in the Trenches

Now we get to the worker bees, the people who do the actual translations. Translators have several people to whom they are responsible and report. Usually, they work in teams, and the team members determine what a word's meaning will be. Sitting a step above the team is the general editor, whose job is to settle any differences and keep traditional thinking in mind. At the head of the table is the group that is paying for the translation. Now we get to see the real power of what a translation will look like, for the money always gets to say how something will look. If you do not believe me, check out the preface or introduction of a given Bible, and you will see the bias of the translation. Is that good or bad? That is not the correct question to ask. What needs to be answered is how it fits into the inerrancy thing that literalists insist on.

Translators, the people who have dedicated their lives to learning and understanding multiple languages and civilizations, do not get enough credit, and upon the publishing of a new or revised translation, get all the hate and vitriol from John Q. Pewsitter if a word or sentence structure has been modified from what they know to be true (tradition).[12] I do not envy the translators, for they are working on documents that have been written over the course of twelve to fifteen hundred years—which ended almost two thousand years ago!

The Hebrew Tanakh, according to critical analysis, was started sometime around the eighth century BCE. The Christian testament was supposedly

---

12   Sadly, there is a whole group of people and churches that insist the King James Version is the only true translation. All other translations are of the devil, and you will go to hell for trusting your soul to them.

canonized[13] at the Council of Hippo in 397 CE, but the actual, official texts were written by the middle of the second century CE. I realize these dates are rough, but no one put a "date published" stamp on any of the works. A translator always wants to get to the earliest text available since this is going to be considered the most dependable as a source document. That makes sense to us, of course. Find the original manuscript, and you have the writer's own intentions without errors, edits, or glosses.[14] No problem, they are all scattered about, right? Wrong! We have no, I repeat *no*, original writing from any of the Hebrew or Christian texts. Here is a bit of history that will highlight this issue.

In 1947, the biblical world was rocked to its core when a kid threw stones into a cave in Qumran, Israel. Here was every archaeologist's dream: a massive trove of biblical writings that dated to the middle of the first century BCE![15] This trove included parts or all of the books of the Tanakh except the book of Ruth. What a find for scholars and translators! Now they could see a thousand years further back in history than before and gain a better understanding of how, or if, texts had changed in the years from the Leningrad Codex creation (ca. 1000 CE). Scholars were amazed to find that scribal errors and glosses were at a minimum. However (isn't there always a however?), there was a problem with one particular book, and that book was Jeremiah. Good old Jeremiah, that wacko codger who named his scribe for us, Baruch ben Neriah.

Why was Jeremiah a problem with our understanding of ancient works and how they should be considered? Let us play a thinking game to understand the dilemma that will follow. Choose a book at random from your local library. In the frontispiece, we see how many various printings and editions there have been since it was originally published. For older books, there will be more. It will increase exponentially with printings in other languages. If one reverses this process, we finally find the original printing house. That printer guarantees there was one single copy that the publisher used as the template. The book of Jeremiah tromps all over our

---

13   An authorized list of books for use in worship.

14   In the biblical world, an original writing is known as an autographic text.

15   Dating of the texts are from the third to the first century BCE.

grand assumption of how things were written, the theory being that if we go farther back in time, we will see fewer and fewer versions of a particular writing. Yet here we have Jeremiah's book, sitting in Qumran for almost two thousand years with a secret.

What is that secret? There are two original books by Jeremiah. Seriously! One is like what we have today (Masoretic) in any Bible you will find, and the other is about an eighth shorter (Septuagint), which is what Jesus and his posse used. Oh, in the longer version (Masoretic), the chapters are not in the same order we read in our daily devotions. Depending on who you read, scholar or theologian, these two versions are either similar or wildly different. And therefore are co-equal—or not. What a kerfuffle, eh? So which version is the correct version? Did Jeremiah's scribe, Baruch ben Neriah, pen a Hemingway-length version and a Reader's-Digest version? Why would that happen? No one really knows.

Above is mentioned the Masoretic text (MS) and the Septuagint (LXX). These two texts are the gold standard for everything we pew warmers know, so spending a bit of time to understand them is important. Start with Alexander the Great's rule of the known world in the fourth century BCE. He commissioned Jewish scholars to translate the Hebrew writings into Greek. We know it today as the Septuagint.[16] We know that Jesus and his followers used this translation for their quotations. The writers of the Gospels and St. Paul used this translation for their prophecy fulfillments. The LXX was also used in the early days of Catholicism to translate the Tanakh into Latin. Yes, it is a very important version, and the oldest version that scholars and translators have is from the middle of the twelfth century CE.

As for the Hebrew Tanakh, until 1947, the oldest text was the Aleppo Codex written circa 930 CE, but it is incomplete, due to a fire. Maimonides (CE 1138–1204), the revered Jewish sage, relied on the Aleppo Codex for authority in his Mishnah Torah. Other famous Jewish sages sang the Aleppo Codex's praise. The Aleppo Codex, the crown jewel, is famed for its accuracy and extensive textual (Masora) notes.

---

16   The Septuagint is also referred to as LXX. Both monikers are Latin, and both mean "seventy." Where the name comes from is a fun bit of trivia, but it has no real basis in fact and will not be discussed here.

The oldest *complete* copy of the Hebrew Tanakh is the Leningrad Codex, known today as the Masoretic text. This book is the standard scholarly text of the Hebrew Bible. If you read a Hebrew or Christian Bible today, it will be translated from the Leningrad Codex.[17] Sadly, this is not considered the best quality manuscript; the Aleppo Codex is best, so the scholars say—but the Masoretic is really, really good. We can thank the Masoretes, a group of scholars who, sometime in the early part of the first millennium, made preserving the Hebrew Tanakh their life's work. Sadly, we do not have any of the original texts they used. Masoretes are to be thanked for their using the creation of Aaron ben Moses ben Asher for the Tiberian system of vowel, punctuation, and accent notes in the margins of the text. We also know Maimonides praised his notation idea and used his authority to promote the new way of notating the texts.

Jumping back into the fray comes biblical criticism (the bane of evangelicals and fundamentalists everywhere, remember?). No, this science is not about theological issues, which is a relief. The scholars, many of whom are Jewish, do the work of linguists. Biblical criticism offers insight into what is gloss, what has been redacted or edited, and what is original. These brilliant people are maligned because they insist on studying the Tanakh and the Christian testament as literary work. This book you are reading would not have been possible without using the techniques and understanding available through the various critical methods.[18]

Now we shall consider another part of the translator's job. Obviously, no language directly imports its word meanings on a one-to-one basis. The translator's job is to take what they think the writer meant, put a spin on it, and write it into the other language. As you can imagine, there will be a lot of bias and meaning added. I am sure most translators attempt to avoid such things, however. Let me offer an instance of just how this works out into the reality of our Bibles today. Consider Genesis 1:21:

---

17   Yes, the Leningrad Codex resides in Leningrad, Russia.

18   Biblical criticism is (1) the *scientific* concern to avoid dogma and bias by applying a neutral, non-sectarian, reason-based judgment to the study of the Bible, and (2) the belief that the reconstruction of the historical events behind the texts, as well as the history of how the texts themselves developed, would lead to a correct understanding of the Bible. (Wikipedia, last edited 13 October 2024, "Biblical criticism," https://en.wikipedia.org/wiki/Biblical_criticism.)

- "And God prepareth the *great monsters*" (YLT).

- "So, God created the *great creatures of the sea*" (NIV).

- "So, God created *great sea animals*" (TLB).

- "And God created *great whales*" (KJV).

Well, which is it? We have been told by today's scholars and pulpit pounders that there is only one true reading, and that is to take the words literally. Is the real, true meaning whales, sea animals, creatures, monsters, or what?[19]

You can even take this example in one of two ways. Is this example nontheological, or does it have a theological bent? Translations can be tricky if you do not know what you are doing. They are tricky even when you *do* know what you are doing! This example has been discussed earlier in the first chapter, so we know the author's writing was a polemic against the Mesopotamian god structure. Therefore, Young's translation is the correct meaning.

Conclusion

If a pastor or church pushes a particular translation, ask why that is. Most important is to read the preface of the translation yourself. This is your life on which you are betting. Get the translation that works for you. Research to your heart's content. I recommend more than one translation, for I use several. Look at the sea monster part above and remind yourself there are numerous sides to a story. Mind also, these stories are so much richer when discovering the surrounding *Sitz im Leben* of the writer's mindset and outlook on what was happening in his own backyard.

Have you wondered why the Scripture references in this book are many and varied? I look for a translation that offers the best idea of the original. On my desk, I have two current translations of the Hebrew Tanakh. Also represented is a current translation of the New Testament from the Greek and a copy of the Septuagint. I refer to several online sources, one of which is an interlinear Tanakh, a vital part of my research. Also found are the great

---

19   The monsters/the great ones (הַתַּנִּינִם הַגְּדֹלִים). From the Hebrew interlinear text.

sagas of Mesopotamia and Ugarit, for these writings are immensely helpful to understand that day's cultural milieu. Writings from the inter-testamental period also add to the understanding of how Jesus and St. Paul thought and acted. Merely reading the sixty-six books found in the Bible strangles one's attempt to glean what meanings are to be found in them.

I will leave you with the words of 2 Timothy 2:15: "Be diligent to present thyself approved to God—a workman irreproachable, rightly dividing the word of the truth" (YLT). It is the responsibility of each person to understand, from whatever source is available, what is important to living a life worth living.

CHAPTER 16

Hard Data on the Flood

This chapter involves considering various physical structures that surround the flood event. We will look at the volume of water necessary to cover the whole earth, what happens when tectonic plates do what they do, and weather happenings that occurred during the end of the last ice age. What happens when vast quantities of water are disturbed? Consideration of animal typology and ancient boats of diverse types are ahead.

Why this science stuff, you ask? To get our minds in the proper frame, we must first set our minds on what is going to be larger than life in the various areas of discussion below. With that in mind, an adjustment is necessary from the start. The ancients' world was catastrophically devastated by a deluge and flood of unimaginable proportions. Their world was utterly destroyed. How would we of today process such a thing? Is it possible to comprehend something on a similar scale? To my mind, there is only one place in our world where you might achieve this level of understanding, and that place is the Grand Canyon. Do not mistake my meaning here; I am not a young earth person who goes gaga over this landmark as proof of the flood. There are so many logic holes in their attempt to use this wonder as their proof—one could hold more water in a sieve than accept the snake oil they are selling.

Rather, let us use the enormity of that geological wonder to grasp the enormity of something else. Go there and look out on the vista. You, after a moment or two, say, "Yes, that is a big hole in the ground." You stay a few days and feel the draw to view it over and over again. People who experience the Grand Canyon in this way realize one does not know how to process the vast spaces and the ageless processes it took to make what they are viewing. You finally realize the proper response to how big the Grand Canyon is: to say you do not know. That hole in the ground occurred over millions of years.[1]

Literalists say it took less than a year. Yeah, right. To understand events that occurred during this flood saga, we must look into the deep, dark annals of the past. Then, we will do something that is absurd for common Bible readers. We will look at the actual words of Genesis and see if what happened was possible.

That will be fun, right?!

Pull Out Your Globe

Anatolia, which is now considered Turkey, butts up to the southern part of the Black Sea. It is separated from Europe to the west by the Aegean Sea and, more important to us, by the Bosphorus Strait. The strait is only nineteen miles long and under a half mile at its narrowest, yet this piece of real estate has had such an impact on human history. Scythians, Hittites, the sea peoples, and traders from time immemorial used it. Persians and Greeks fought over its control, as did Christians and the Saracens. WWII saw it hamper Allied forces. Genghis Khan rode around it. It is as important to much of the world as the Suez or Panama Canals are to us in the United States. Its creation is also what brings us the formation for our quest today.

The eastern part of Turkey is bounded by the Greater Caucasus and Lesser Caucasus Mountain ranges. To the west and south are the Taurus Mountains, where the headwaters of the Tigris and Euphrates Rivers form. Looking north from Mesopotamia (east of Israel), their northeastern side is bounded by the Kurdistan and Zagros Mountain ranges, which adjoin the

---

1   David Montgomery, 2012, *The Rocks Don't Lie*, W.W. Norton & Co.

Lesser Caucasus range. Directly to the north and east of Mesopotamia are the Taurus mountains, which the Tigris and Euphrates flow through, finally reaching the flood plain for where our story will occur. It is here we can look back and see a possibility for what caused both flood events.

Our weather patterns for the Black Sea are easterly, from the Bosphorus Strait across to the Caucasus Mountains. There, they are bent one of three ways, north above the Greater Caucasus along the Manych Spillway.[2] They also flow straight through the valley between the Caucasus mountains. Most of the weather flows eastward from the Bosphorus Straight, passing over the Black Sea toward the Caucasus Mountain ranges. This pattern turns southeast along the mountain ranges just to the north of Mesopotamia. All this waters the eastern portion of the Euphrates and into the mountains that now separate Iraq and Iran.

What is normally thought of as Mesopotamia resides between the two rivers, Tigris to the east, and the Euphrates to the west. Our two rivers join up above the Persian Gulf and empty into that gulf. All water that forms and falls in the Caucasus region up north will follow these rivers to the sea. Mesopotamia is one vast flood plain. It is a perfect location for migrants, for it has rich soil and other desirable resources. And doom—big catastrophic, mind-numbing doom.

Ice, Ice, Baby

At the end of the last ice age, worldwide sea levels rose and rose fast.[3] We know sea levels rose because the Mediterranean Sea created the Dardanelles Strait, which formed the Sea of Marmara to its north. Continuing water level risings caused the creation and excavation of the Bosphorus Strait, which inundated the Black Sea. It did not stop there. Still rising, waters passed north again, through the Kerch Strait, forming the Sea of Azov. With water still rising, it flowed north again across the Manych Spillway, reshaping the Caspian Sea. Put simply, massive amounts of water reshaped the geography north of Mesopotamia in less than two years.

---

2   Manych Spillway is how the Caspian Sea was inundated when the Black Sea flooded.
3   Approximately 6800 BCE.

This caused massive weather upheavals to the south, right into our target area. This is nice and proper to know, but we will focus only on one event, the inundation of the Black Sea via the Bosphorus Strait. The start of the process we are considering was the collapse of the Laurentide Ice Sheet.[4] This caused a quick jump in the sea levels. Remember science class? The oceans are connected, and water seeks its own level. When the Pacific, Atlantic, or Indian Ocean levels rise, the Mediterranean Sea rises as well. The Sea of Marmara, which is part of the Mediterranean Sea, rose enough to overflow its banks through what is now known as the Bosphorus Strait.

The resulting outlay of seawater reached ten cubic miles of water a day, two hundred times the flow of Niagara Falls! This inundation lasted, at minimum, for one year. The channel cut by that torrent resulted in the Bosphorus Strait being, on average, several hundred feet deep. That, my friend, is a lot of water! It caused massive flooding along the coastline of the already full Black Sea. The coastline was expanded by miles daily. It is calculated that more than ninety-three thousand miles of land was submerged, about the land mass of the United Kingdom.

Have you ever been to Niagara Falls or any other waterfall? Of course, the water goes over the edge and plunks down on the rocks below, but what is fascinating and integral to our story is the plume of mist that is formed. Imagine such a spray from something two hundred times in size to Niagara Falls, such as the creation of the Bosphorus Strait. The enormous flood of watery mist caused the air to be supersaturated, and the prevailing winds caused the moisture to follow east until it came into contact with the mountain ranges to the east. Warm Mediterranean air meets colder mountain air. The result was a cataclysmic precipitation event unknown before its time or since.

I find it hard to imagine, even with reading the Genesis account and the *Epic of Gilgamesh*. Imagine, if possible, a large body of water being expanded unimaginably fast, which caused a precipitation deluge of mind-blowing proportions. Into a region filled with mountainous terrain. With rainfall in

4   The Laurentide ice sheet covered much of North America during the Pleistocene period. At our point in history, there was a massive melting and calving of this ice. The very rapid melting is what caused the raising of the world's ocean levels.

volumes never seen before, the flooding of the lower valleys broke through the natural dams and flooded even more valleys. Lower peaks were submerged, which led to those mountains coming apart. Finally, this assault of water merged with several of the headwaters of the two above-mentioned rivers. Layer upon layer of water finally resulted in an unprecedented overflowing of two or more rivers, which devastated the whole of the mountainous environments they traversed. This deluge traveled south toward the Persian Gulf, wiping away people, animals, cities, farms, crops, and creepy crawlies. Even the topography was altered.

Myth tells us all that was saved from this destruction was one family and some animals.

Literally Speaking

According to biblical literalists, those who accept the world being created from nothing in six days, accept the literal flooding of the whole of the earth, rising twenty-two feet above every mountain. That, my friends, is a lot of water, and credulity is stretched far past the breaking point. So I did the math. Truthfully, I got a physicist to help me, since there were funny letters, differential calculus, numbers higher than my fingers and toes combined, pi, average sizes of various parts of the earth, and the possibility of the Cubs winning the World Series to contend with.[5] The basic idea was how much water had to be present to rise twenty-two feet above Mount Everest (29,319 feet above mean sea level) since that is the literal understanding that must be considered. We know from the Noah saga that all the water came not just from the sky but from inside the earth.

> In the six hundredth year of Noah's life, in the second month, on the seventeenth day of the month, *on the same day all the fountains of the great deep burst open*, and the floodgates of the sky were opened. The rain fell upon the earth for forty days and forty nights. —Genesis 7:11–12 (NASB)

Here we encounter the phenomenon of waters coming from under the earth. Where and why did the writer think devastating flooding came from

---

5   That physicist is my son, who is an admirable person. Well-liked by friends and all his students. My thanks to you, Tyler, for your guidance and knowledge.

under the earth? Take your twenty-first-century glasses off and put your way-back glasses on. Pause for a moment and turn to the graphic at the end of this chapter.[6] What is shown is the cosmic map that purported to be the reality until some guy pointed a telescope into the night sky. Ancient people had a different perspective of the world compared to us. Note what is under the palm trees in the center of the image. These are the Lower Waters, the primordial waters. What might those primordial waters be? The logic of the lower waters was that creation caused the dry land to separate from the waters, which were held there by the pillars of the earth. The water we see in the oceans, seas, and lakes is a part of the original primordial water, with dry land resting on top.

> Then God said, *"Let the waters below the heavens* be gathered into one place, and let the dry land appear"; and it was so. And God called the dry land "earth," and the gathering of the waters He called "seas"; and God saw that it was good. —vv. 9–10 (NASB)
>
> You shall not make for yourself a carved image, or any likeness of what is in heaven above or on the earth beneath or *in the water under the earth.* —Deuteronomy 5:8 (NASB)
>
> God spread out *the earth upon the waters.* —Psalm 136:6 (NASB)
>
> He has founded it (dry land) *upon the seas* and established it upon the rivers. —Psalm 24:2 (NASB)

Here is where the waters came from in the Noah story. Please understand also that this cosmic map was considered the truth, the whole truth, and nothing but the truth at the time. Moses, Jesus, Alexander the Great, Archimedes, Julius Caesar, and our most ancient forbearer, Glog. Every one of these people knew the cosmos was built in the fashion seen in that drawing. We know today, however, that the dry land rests, not on the primordial waters, but on the earth's mantle, which overlays the outer core, which encircles the inner core of the earth. Of course, you say, "Anyone with half a brain can easily see there is a lot of earth. There is an average of 6,357 kilometers from sea level to the center of the earth, and water could easily be hidden inside all that great cubic volume."

---

6   Dickin, Alan P., 2002, Biblical and ancient Near Eastern worldview, *On a Faraway Day … : A New View of Genesis in Ancient Mesopotamia*, Brentwood Christian Press.

The only problem is that the crust of the earth is the only place where water might be hidden. The crust is a very thin segment, ranging from twenty kilometers to only three kilometers. Due to temperature, gravity, and composition, the mantle, inner, and outer cores are physically incapable of containing water. Taking this into account, to achieve a worldwide flood of such proportions, the assumed extra water would require the crust itself to be over 70 percent water. Think about this for a moment. For this to be true, all the mountains, hills, deserts, arable land, and volcanic peaks have to be supersaturated with water. We have an English word for such a physical manifestation—it's called a marsh. Marshes are not found everywhere, and certainly not on mountains or in deserts. Definitely not near a volcano! The water in marshy areas is represented in the catalog of freshwater amounts worldwide. Our resource for the numbers used? We took the figures to calculate from the National Oceanic and Atmospheric Administration (NOAA).

Literalists insist they are right in their literalism, and so fantasize that the face of the earth was flat. They claim the mountains rose due to the tidal stresses from the flood. Their claim is because of their version of scientific trickery that is, in a loose way, based on actual science. This is their escape route, for if the world were flat, then yes, the world's water supply could cover the earth—except for one tiny, inconsequential item. The earth's water supply can only do that if *the entire world were flat*, including the ocean depths. When approached regarding this problem, they shout, *"Squirrel!"* and rush to change the subject.

Waves, Big Waves

Next, we need to take into consideration what happens to water when land interferes with it dynamically. Do this—fill your bathtub with water. Using your spouse's favorite large cooking pot, push it quickly into the tub of water. What happens? After all the splashing stops, pull the pot out just as quickly. Again, what happens? On a worldwide scale, we call these watery happenings tidal waves, or tsunamis. That pot is pretending to be a landmass. That bathtub full of water is the earth's oceans. Imagine this on the scale of the world. What size waves will there be when California falls into the Pacific Ocean?

Scale that up to entire continents doing the same thing simultaneously. You must not forget the oceans getting deeper concurrently. Are you willing to actually believe a boat the size of the Ark (or any boat or yellow submarine) would survive? We look down at the deepest parts of the oceans, awestruck by their depths. Looking up instead of down, the world's mountain ranges would have risen by a great margin. Go back to your bathtub experiment. With a friend and another of your spouse's favorite pots that is even larger, push both pots down *and* up simultaneously. Tsunami versus boat, no imagination needed who will win. Yet literalists think our two arks survived this? The literalist science is silly.

Round or Square

I mention again the construction of the arks as represented in the two sagas. Noah's boat was a rectangle—no pointy ends as represented at the YE Creation Museum. Sorry artists, you lose out on this one. Utna'pishtim's ark was round. This difference has caused preachers and Sunday school teachers to mock Utna'pishtim's boat. "What a stupid way to build a boat! No one in their right mind builds a round boat. This proves their story is made up!" And yet—

> Round boats are a fascination, and the quffa, a basket-built boat from Iraq, is among the most fascinating because of its well-documented antiquity, its common use well into the 20th century, and its sometimes very large— occasionally immense—size. Known also as a kuphar and by various alternate spellings, the quffa was described in the fifth century BCE by Herodotus, who stated that they were built in Armenia for one-way trading trips on the Euphrates.[7]

There is a cuneiform tablet from Babylon, dating to around 1750 BCE and discovered in the 1940s, that describes a world-inundating flood in a clear precursor to the story of Noah. In this version, the god Enki clues a man named Atra'hasis to the coming disaster and suggests he build a quffa to save himself.

---

7   Indigenous Boats, April 16, 2016, "The Mesopotamian Quffa or Kuphar," https://indigenousboats.blogspot.com/2016/04/the-mesopotamian-quffa-or-kuphar.html.

The quffa, or coracle, as the British say, is what Utna'pishtim built and used. The ark of Noah takes its shape from being so close to the Mediterranean Sea, where round boats did not work well. Are these two watercraft the same, but different? Yes, they are, for regional differences, but *only skin deep, as the saying goes.*

Go back to our bathtub experiment. This is a microcosm of what tremendous waves do. Those waves would not notice a rectangular boat five hundred feet in length, or Utna'pishtim's round boat with about the same cubic space. Literalists disregard this point of view because it makes them look silly. I have one further point of logistics regarding these epics (this discussion will be short): the only real problem is that the two crafts, Noah's or Utna'pishtim's craft, went north, as the flood stories suggest when the waters receded. If we take these sagas as written, the craft used to save the heroes was built hundreds of miles to the south from where they eventually settled. In that part of the world, water flows to the south. How did those boats, which had *no steering capabilities*, end in the far north? Here, we must get metaphysical. The far north, to the people of that age, is where the gods lived, for those were the closest, highest peaks known at that time. *Hmmm.*

Noah was six hundred years old when the flood happened. Before the flood story, we read the lineage from Adam to Noah, with everyone living about as long as it takes for the Chicago Cubs to win the World Series (hundreds and hundreds of years). "So what, all these early guys were old, big deal." Yes, it was a big deal to the redactor, and here is when and why we know this. When is easy, for this addition is being written by the same person who penned our first creation story. Ezra is using the Hebrew origin stories to refute the origin stories of Babylon, where he had been living not too long before. His play on Noah's age is slick but simple. I am sure his readers were chuckling as they read and got the underlying polemic.

Hidden Numbers

Want to know what the joke is? Of course you do. The Babylonian numbering system is a base 60. Today, we use a base 10 for counting. Have you ever wondered why our clocks are 60 minutes per hour? Why are there 360 degrees in a circle? The divisors for 10 are 1, 2, 5, and 10. Divisors for 60 are 1, 2, 3, 5, 6, 10, 12, 15, 30, and 60. With base 60, you are able to define something with far more accuracy. Next, Noah's age is the complete number 60, times 10. The redactor's audience got the joke without having to think about it. To reiterate an example, if you are a sports person and hear the term "carrying the rock," your mind instantly knows this refers to football. Remember, if you will, Utna'pishtim, Noah's Mesopotamian counterpart, is the Akkadian translation of *Ziusudra*. He is the last king named in the Sumerian King List who lived before the flood. Ziusudra is the tenth king on the list. Noah is the tenth ancestor of Adam before the flood. Ezra, with an economy of words, directed his readers toward this exact point—Noah is Utna'pishtim! As the story unfolds, we also see that after the flood, Ezra's god remakes the world, much as he did the first time around, with the same promise to Noah as he offered to Adam.

Counting the Animals

When attempting to count the animals that came on the ark, we find a bit of a slap-fight between the compiler and the redactor. Ask anyone today how many of each animal Noah took on the ark, and you will get the answer: two of each (a pair). Yet upon reading the story, seven pairs of clean animals are mentioned as having boarding passes for the cruise. Which number is correct, two or seven? Two, male and female, is obvious. More important to our discussion, the original oral mythos our compiler used required only a pair for propagation of the species after the flood. Our redactor comes along with a different approach to this topic. Due to the time frame of the redaction, Noah used the extra five clean animals to use as an offering of thanks to his god. This is another important clue to his work, for Utna'pishtim did the same thing, but as an appeasement to the gods. In actuality, for Utna'pishtim, it was more of an apology for not dying like the rest of humanity. In his time, our redactor knew that an offering of thanks, not appeasement, was necessary, so he added a few more animals to the list. So, yes, there are both two and seven pairs of certain animals on the ark. Now you know!

Looking at Rocks

Arizona is rife with geological wonders. The actions of plate tectonics have raised, lowered, stretched, and riddled the landscape. Tucson sits in the middle of a vast extinct caldera. Signs of the earth that stretched are obvious to anyone who drives through this part of Southern Arizona. Not far north of Phoenix, the earth rises rather abruptly at the Mogollon Rim, which stretches across the state. On top of the Rim to the east is the Petrified Forest.[8] Hundreds of millennia ago, this whole area was a lush forest that had been swallowed up by the sea for centuries, which turned the trees into rocks. During this time, northern Arizona went through upheavals, unlike the south of the state. Here to the north, the land rose. The western part of the state is taken up by the Grand Canyon. Over six thousand feet at its deepest, this immense gash in the earth shows a history of how this part of Arizona was formed. Take a trek up from the bottom, and you will see outlines of the many eons of different sedimentary happenings. In this microcosm, one can only hope to grasp the concept of how old this planet is.

Literalists insist, however, that all of what makes the Grand Canyon so old was done during the flood (five thousand-ish years ago). The logic of that argument fails on so many levels that it is difficult to consider them all. I will speak to the most glaring problem, however. The canyon, from top to bottom, is made of numerous layers of sediment that have been heated and compressed into rock. To make sediment into rock requires not only heat and compression but a vast amount of time. Five thousand years is nowhere near enough to do the work. With that in mind, pretend the Grand Canyon was formed during the flood and the waters from that event as they flowed away, creating that whole great gash. If this were true, the earth would be mud. Mud washes away easily, which is not seen in the canyon. The evidence is that the Colorado River has etched its way down through the rock over eons. It cannot have been created by a flood, even of one of epic proportions.

---

8   The average elevation in the Petrified Forest is over one mile above sea level.

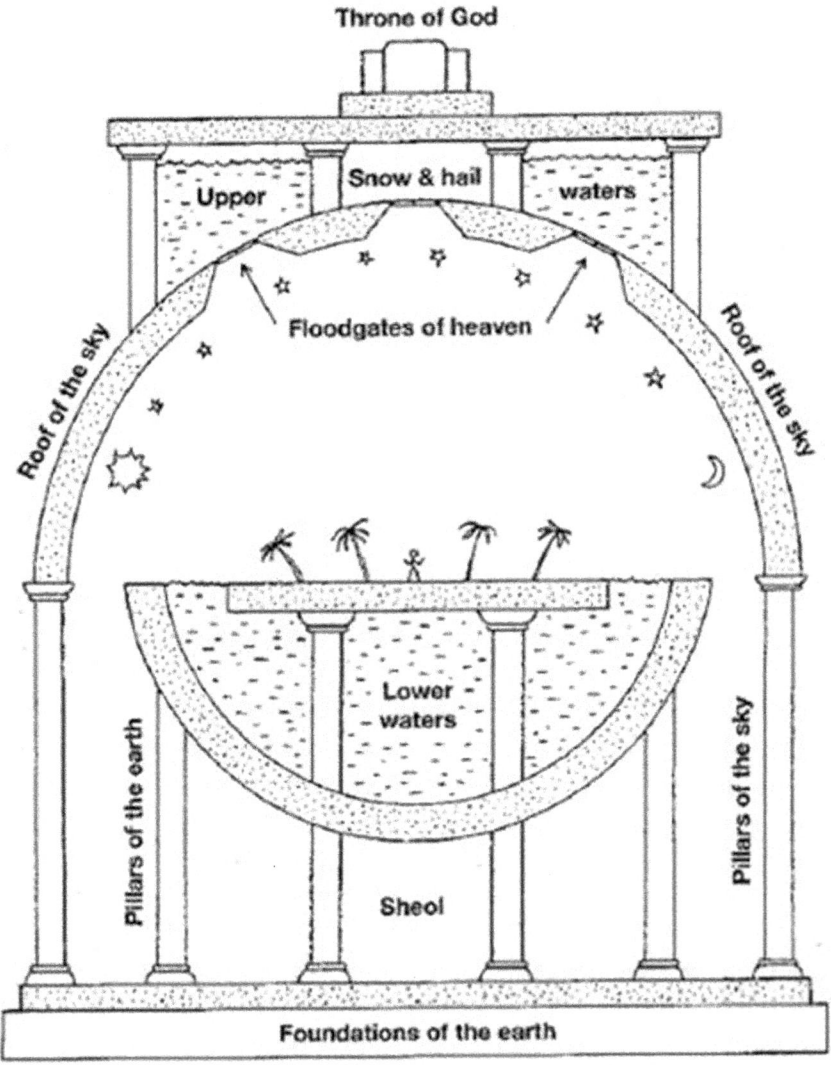

CHAPTER 17

I See Dead People[1]

Written twenty-five centuries ago, the accepted theory is those ancient authors did not have the intrinsic ability to put a long-form storyline together because the art of writing was so new. Yet, over and over again, this opinion is destroyed. The Sumerian and Mesopotamian creation epics are yet more proof of ancient stories being exciting, captivating one's imagination, and inviting the reader along for the ride. I am reminded of the subtlety and creativeness found in the later sagas of Homer, thought to be written in the eighth century BCE. And of Beowulf written at the turn of the tenth century CE. Not only were these epics penned but penned in poetic (rhyming) form—not in a straight narrative style. We, in the twenty-first century, look at ancient works and, without even reading them, deride their inherent creativity and style.

I disagree with that poor assessment of earlier works wholeheartedly. Over and over in this book, we see an abundance of written artistry that rivals any book written since. I did, however, keep running past the Adamic and Noahide genealogies in Genesis. We have two lists of people having babies— big deal. Such a thing does not fit into any role seen so far. They are boring and mundane to our twenty-first-century minds. Scholars say there is no

---

1   I want to give acknowledgment to three authors whose works were instrumental in my understanding of how this chapter worked out: Umberto Cassuto, Hermann Gunkel, and Claus Westermann.

definitive reason the two lineages are necessary. Or if there is a reason, how the passages make any sense of how they are presented.[2]

This did not sit well with me. I have such deep respect for what has been uncovered so far in this book. There must be a purpose and plan for the lineages. So I started again. I found the key. It is startling and audacious! What is uncovered hearkens clear back to the first creation story. It gives an insight into something referred to in the Exodus saga that, upon first reading, has no real impact. We also get to consider yet again the goings-on in the first creation story that require genealogies to appear. Excellent!

Lineage Archaeology

Let us consider genealogies. We are told there are two lineages in Genesis. First is the Adamic tradition (see Genesis 5). We then see the Noahide Table of Nations (see Genesis 10). Preached far and wide as being the only two, this is, however, a misnomer. Looking closer, we find nine (nine!) family trees in Genesis.

1. Cain's family tree (see Genesis 4:17–24)
2. Adam to Noah (see Genesis 5)
3. Noah's Table of Nations (see Genesis 10)
4. Shem's descendants—Canaan, Mesopotamia (see Genesis 11:10)
5. Terah to Abraham (see Genesis 11:27–32)
6. Lot's lineage—Ammonites, Moabites (see Genesis 19:36–38)
7. Ishmael—Arabs, and Isaac's kin (see Genesis 25:12–18)
8. The children of Israel—Jacob's progeny (see Genesis 29:31–30:23)
9. Esau's family tree—Edomites (see Genesis 36)

Well, this is a fine mess. What am I supposed to do with my brilliant idea now? Invoking my rat terrier persona, I started digging. I discounted the whole "years lived" thing in the Adamic genealogy. This is a transparent reference to the Sumerian Kings List.[3] I did not know why Seth's family line was here,

---

2   The most accepted idea is that Ezra used genealogies to move time along quickly.

3   We know well by now that Ezra was not afraid to use Babylonian ideas to suit his purpose. The SKL is a great starting point, though it will not be delved into because it is not germane to the topic.

and I was not interested. I did see people "begetting" and "knowing" one's wife, good for them—healthy fertility happening back in the day. There was technological innovation and nation-building going on. Yay for civilization and technology!

As I looked at these family trees, I grew concerned about why only two of them are considered in religious circles. Those two are the Sethian list and Noahide Table of Nations. Why only these two? What caused the other lineages to be discarded from conversation? If we read about the progenitor or the relationship to Adonai's people and consider a bit, the answer becomes apparent.

- **Cain**—This one is easy, for he is a very bad man, verboten and yucky. He killed his brother, so anything he or his progeny did was bad by default. Even though the technology introduced by his line is fantastic and in use today, we discard them with a sniff and snort. This must be true, for I have heard it from the pulpit.

- **Esau**—Isaac's older brother, the redhead who cannot catch a break. The firstborn of twins who got screwed out of his birthright and blessing by the antics of his mother and twin. His brother, Jacob, is the person of interest in this duet, for Jacob's twelve sons go on to fame and fortune. Edom, Esau's line, has justifiable enmity toward the nation of Israel. Esau's family was instrumental in the fall of Judah and the destruction of the first temple.[4]

- **Ishmael**—Abraham's first firstborn son. His lineage is ignored because we are not concerned with his story, for the Hebrew history is interested in the second firstborn of Abraham. Ishmael becomes the father of what will become the Arab nation and the third religion from Abraham's seed. An interesting factoid that is never spoken of was that he fathered twelve sons like his brother from another mother.

- **Lot**—We do not speak of his line since his progeny came from having sex with his daughters (yikes!). From this incest came the nations of Ammon and Moab. Not much about Ammon is mentioned, but we

---

4   The prophet Obadiah spent his whole spittle-laced book castigating Edom. Edom's press secretary must be so proud.

find enmity between Moab and Israel. Historically, Israel did a very good job of mistreating the Moabites. The Moabites escaped the clutches of Israel after King Ahab died.[5]

- **Shem**—Considering where his family created their safe space, we find they were the original crew that populated both Canaan and Mesopotamia. Both these areas will become vitally important later in the Bible. Canaan is where Abraham settled in after fleeing Mesopotamia, and the land the children of Israel had to conquer after the exodus saga. Mesopotamia is where the Hebrew people were exiled after Nebuchadnezzar destroyed both the Northern Kingdom and Southern Kingdom.

- **Terah**—He is only important because he fathered Abram (Abraham).

There we have a synopsis of the genealogies in Genesis that were ignored. Other than interesting tidbits, I found nothing to sink my teeth into, no hook that would render the substance of why these lineages were included in Genesis.

Creation Surprise

As I researched, the first creation story began to show its muscle. A problem that had been vexing me was why the actions of each day were ordered the way they were. I eventually saw a foundation, a rationale, if you will, in and for the creation sequence. The light bulb turned on. What had been hidden right in front of my eyes became obvious. There was a reason for the order in which things were created! Consider the two words *mobility* and *fecundity*, as they pertain to each storyline. The next shoe to drop is the understanding of the *real meaning* of why the statements *be fruitful and multiply* (or words to that effect), were placed where they were. This directive was toward those creations where fertility was denoted. Fish, sea monsters, birds, creepy crawlies, and the beasts of the field are directed to "teem after their kind." Included also were grass, herbs, and trees, to bring forth after their kind. The Cosmic Creator God finished with:

> And God blessed them, saying, "*Be fruitful, and multiply*, and fill the waters in the seas, and the fowl let multiply in the earth." —Genesis 1:22 (NET)

---

5   No white whales were harmed or involved in that dispute.

But wait, there's more! On the sixth day, the Cosmic Creator God made male and female—in his image. And then his command to them ups the ante from his directive to the other fertile creations. Be fruitful and multiply. The Cosmic Creator God says the same words to every living thing created. He adds one additional directive to the man and woman: subdue the earth.

> God blessed them and said to them, "*Be fruitful and multiply! Fill the earth and subdue it!* Rule over the fish of the sea and the birds of the air and every creature that moves on the ground." Then God said, "I now give you every seed-bearing plant on the face of the entire earth and every tree that has fruit with seed in it. They will be yours for food. And to all the animals of the earth, and to every bird of the air, and to all the creatures that move on the ground—everything that has living breath in it—I give every green plant for food." It was so.—Genesis 1:28–30 (NET)

Sidebar

Ignore the silliness that has been attached to the last line in the statement, for it has nothing to do with the man and woman only eating vegetarian until Noah gets the pass for omnivores in his story. The Cosmic Creator God is giving man and woman carte blanche to enjoy all the other creations in order to live life fully. Please do not think that I am denigrating plant-based diets. Nor am I making light of caring for the earth and its resources. I honor those who, for nonpolitical reasons, are unable, for whatever reason, to have meat or dairy pass their lips. More power to them for their choice of what to put in their bodies if it helps them lead fuller, richer lives. As for those who desecrate mother earth willingly and without regard, I have no love lost for you. Personally, Mother Nature is a gift that humankind can never copy or replicate. If cognizant of that ideal, this blue marble we live on will last forever, which it will. Only without us if we continue our destructive path.

Back on Path

When considering the genealogies in Genesis, we see the directive be fruitful and multiply being fulfilled. The nine lineages listed above are proof of the directive working. Humankind is being fruitful and multiplying! Families are becoming clans. Clans are morphing not only into tribes but into nations.

What nations offer is an expansion of people out into the world. That, my friends, is one aspect of subduing the earth as the Cosmic Creator God intended!

Consider what else is offered when pondering this fruitful multiplication. The second creation story started with Adam and Eve in a safe space, the Garden of Eden. Protection and food were found in an area separated from the unknown. After being kicked out of the garden (which was, in reality, their god's temple), Adam and Eve got the privilege of creating a garden for their family. As the family multiplied, that family separated to gain more space for fruitful living. Over time (years, decades, millennia—who cares?) the safe space grew. The garden grew. More of earth's face was subdued for the benefit of humankind. Again, subduing the earth occurred.

I want to backtrack and consider how the directive to the fish, birds, beasts, and growing things is in play. Why did the Cosmic Creator God give all categories of living things the same directive, to be fruitful and multiply? Anyone? Class? Bueller? If humankind is to multiply, there must be foodstuffs available to sustain the expanding garden.

Wow—all these years, this is right in front of my eyes, and I did not see the obvious. My bad. Now, consider how intricate the interaction is between not just species but between the flora and fauna. A plant puts out seeds for the birds to eat. The undigested seeds are eliminated elsewhere, allowing that plant to enlarge its reach. And so on. Plants and animals found the world over are there to provide humankind with the resources necessary to follow our directive.

I See More Dead People

As stated above, we only hear of two genealogies talked about in theological circles. Those two are Adam's lineage and Noah's Table of Nations.[6] Sadly, tradition has asked and answered the wrong questions, for what is said has nothing to do with what the author intended for us to know. This should be obvious to the reader, for we of today want to read it as if it was written only

---

6   Again, Genesis 5 and Genesis 10, respectively.

yesterday and not twenty-five centuries ago. Noah's lineage, simply put, outlines and shapes the world as it was known at that time. It is etiology. Adam's progeny is different yet needs to be associated with Cain's lineage to be understood. Preachers and Sunday school teachers refuse to consider anything to do with Cain since he is a bad guy. It is precisely due to that reasoning that it must be considered, and so we shall.

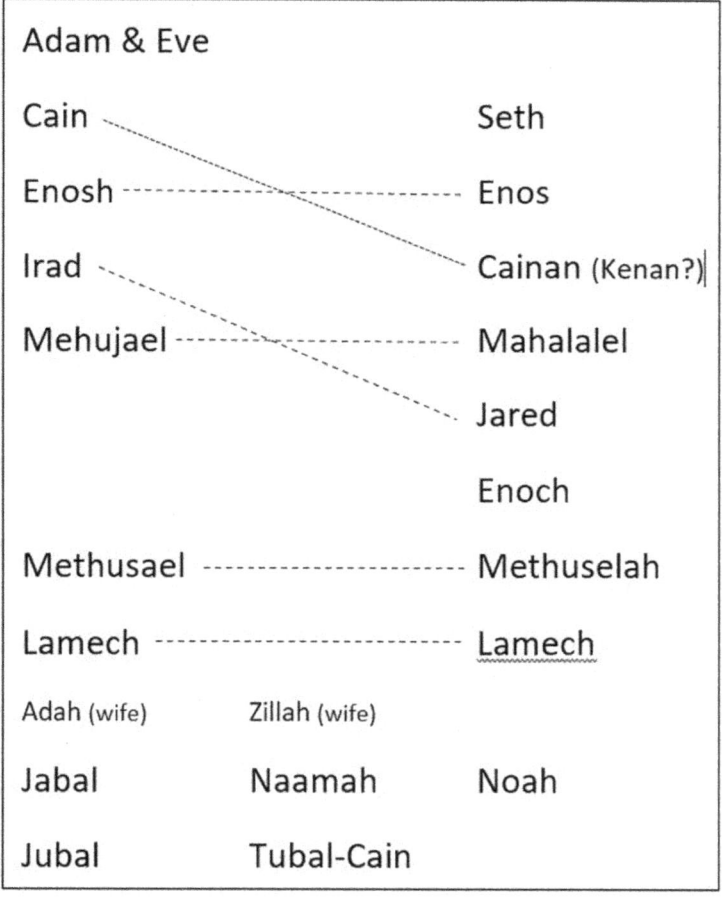

Here we see the two lineages side by side. Without the bias of tradition, one sees the similarities of the people and names associated. One must remember that words were often spelled phonetically until Samuel Johnson's dictionary in 1746. These are the same, with the exception of Cainan and Enoch. A complete mythology has arisen around Enoch throughout the centuries.

Also Known As

Cainan is found both in the antediluvial and post-diluvial lineages. The name is also found in Luke's genealogy of Jesus. Not only that, but he somewhere gets an alias, Kenan. Kenan or Cainan is used, depending on what text you read, in what genealogy, and who is writing. One of those two names might or might not be there. If one reads the Septuagint, Cainan is the name listed in the antediluvial lineup.[7] For the post-diluvian works, the name Kenan is sometimes there, and other times not. Kenan is found in the Septuagint, the Book of Jubilees, and in Luke's genealogy of Jesus. He, however, does not appear in the Masoretic texts, nor in the Samaritan Pentateuch.[8] He is also ignored in the writings of Josephus. Most likely, his story is a fiction created during the late Second Temple period (500–100 BCE).

Our crucial questions are why the name changes from Cainan to Kenan, and what does the name *Cainan* mean to want to change it to something else? One answer is to create an etiology for the Kenite tribe in the far south of Canaan. Located in the Negev desert, this is the place where Moses' father-in-law, Jethro, was a shepherd and priest. Cain has been associated with this tribe for the similarity of the names that are phonetically similar in Hebrew. The name change seems to have happened during or after the exile, and during the Second Temple period (500–100 BCE), for purposes that are not clear. *Cainan* is pronounced kee-nan, which allows for the name to be transformed into *Kenan* over time. *Cain* means spear, but when the verb ending -an (one who creates) is added, the word becomes "smith," one who creates spear (heads). Kenan is, according to scholars, defined in the same way.

Why Cainan/Kenan is placed into the Adamic line is unknown to scholars. It is interesting to note that absolutely no scholarship has been produced questioning this when the other names in Adam's lineage are critiqued. Cain was a farmer who was evicted from the Garden of Eden and eventually bore a son, Enosh, who created the first city. Down the line, we see another name, Tubal-Cain, who makes tools of bronze and iron. Is Cain actually in Seth's lineage? And for what reason? Sadly, we do not know, but it is suspicious that it has never been addressed.

---

7   See Genesis 5:9–13; 1 Chronicles 1:2; Luke 3:37.

8   Both of these texts are considered the best Hebrew writings and are used as the basis for the majority of English translations today.

Looking Under the Hood

Another interesting fact about these two lineages is that we see Lamech as being the last male mentioned in both lines. It is either a one-in-a-million chance[9] to have two fathers in the same place with the same name, or Lamech is the father of Jubal, Jabal, Naamah, and Tubal-Cain, *as well as Noah.* Am I saying what you think? Are these two distinct family lines two different sides of the same coin? Yes, yes, I am. The people are the same, as is the primary father, Adam. Here is the fun part: they are both polemics but pointed toward different purposes.

Cain's lineage was written first and presents the idea of technology as bad. More to the point, it reflects on the idea of city-building (ordered civilization), metalworking, and artistry. These ideas did not come forth from the Garden of Eden where they could be used in wise ways, but rather from a flawed man's mind. These creations ended poorly in the flood (supposedly). Seth's line shows how mankind kept true to their god as evidenced by their long lives and fulfilling the god's command to be fruitful and multiply and subdue the earth. We see the seventh of the line, Enoch, who walked with God and was no more after 365 years.[10] Noah is a godly man who found favor in the sight of his god and was blameless among his contemporaries.[11]

Where is the polemic in Seth's line if they did what they were supposed to do? Here we find another writer, someone who has spent much time in Babylon and knows their story about their pre-flood heroes. We have experienced Ezra's work in Genesis 1, putting his god up against the gods of Babylon. Here he does the same thing, and, as usual, preachers and Sunday school teachers either do not talk about it or get it wrong when they do.

Ezra's Archery Again

Archbishop James Ussher, in his failed attempt to find out when the whole creation thing happened, spent much time in this section. Unfortunately for him, he did not have the information we have today. He did his thing in the 1600s. The Sumerian King List (SKL) was found ca. 1890 and published in

---

9   Which usually happens one out of ten times.

10   The wording in Genesis 6:24 is similar to 2 Kings 2:10 when Elijah departs from the earth.

11   See Genesis 6:8–9.

1906. The similarities between the two lineages are striking but are not the same. For that reason, most evangelicals mock the SKL and disregard the implications, much to the detriment of pew sitters everywhere.

The Adamic line in Genesis 5 is a direct polemic against the SKL. Ezra's hand is as present in this writing as it is in Genesis 1, which is a polemic against the Babylonian creation story, *Enuma Elish*. Ezra wrote during the late exile period (ca. 540 BCE), which is when he penned his Genesis portions. The SKL's oldest written parts are dated to ca. 2084 BCE. Remember, Ezra was part of the Babylonian elite, a scribe and known sage during his life. He knew his Jewish history and rebelled against the Babylonian stories. His god was greater than Marduk and posse, so he wrote against their myths.

Here are the places where the comparison is linked:

1. In the SKL, eight names are listed in the chronology prior to the flood. In the SKL, these are kings of city-states and regions. Genesis lists men, normal, regular men from Adam to Noah. Considering what is different, the SKL does not include the first man or the hero of the flood, which the Adamic line does. We are left with the same construction, however.

2. The men in both lists have abnormally long lives, which is the subject of link number five.

3. In each of the lists, the seventh (En-men-dur-Anna and Enoch) did not die, but ascended into heaven.[12] Both of these men were very close to their god, which is the reason for their removal from the human plane.

4. Both lists have the last entry as the person who survived the flood (Utna'pishtim, king of Shuruppak, and Noah).

5. The years are based on the Babylonian numerical base of 60 in their counting, which is the Babylonian (and Akkadian and Sumerian) versus our base 10, which makes for interesting and humorous attempts to decipher what is going on.

---

12   En-men-dur-Anna ascended into heaven. Enoch walked with God and was no more.

Antediluval Kings List		Genesis 5	
		Adam	930
A-lulim(ak)	28,000	Seth	912
Alalgar	36,000	Enosh	905
En-men-lu-Anna(ak)	43,200	Kenan	910
En-men-gal-Anna(ak)	28,800	Mahalalel	895
Dumu-zi(d)	36,000	Jared	962
En-sip(d)-zi(d)-Anna(k)	28,800	Enoch	365
En-men-dur-Anna(k)	21,000	Methuselah	969
Ubar-Tutu(k)	18,600	Lamech	777
		Noah	950

The kings listed in the SKL are considered demigods—part divine, part human—and are linked with various mythologies of the pre-flood period. We will not consider the numerology behind their extensive years but will consider how the Torah treats Adam's lineage. As said above, these are men, not gods or demigods but men who took advantage of the offer of their god and put that offer to good use. That is stated quietly and without pretension. They were born, begot sons and daughters, and died. Enoch is the only one who gets special treatment, but it is focused on his walk with his god. Consider the table below.

	1st Son	Til Death	Total		1st Son	Til Death	Death	Total
Adam	130	800	930	Adam	30+100	800	30+900	930
Seth	105	807	912	Seth	5+100	7+800	2+10+900	912
Enosh	90	815	905	Enosh	90	5+10+800	5+900	905
Kenan	70	840	910	Cainan	70	40+800	10+900	910
Mahalalel	65	830	895	Mahalel	5+60	30+800	2+60+800	895
Jared	162	800	962	Jared	2+60+100	800	2+60+900	962
Enoch	65	300	365	Enoch	5+60	300	5+60+300	365
Methuselah	187	782	969	Methuselah	7+80+100	2+80+700	9+60+900	969
Lamech	182	595	777	Lamech	2+80+100	5+90+500	7+70+700	777
Noah	500		500	Noah	500	[450]	[950]	950
Until Flood	100	350	950					

The left list is what is seen in any of the Bibles out today. Upon even a short perusal, the first item noticed is that many of the numbers end with zero or five. The other numbers are multiples of five with the addition of seven! Methuselah is special, for he gets two sevens added to his age. To understand what is happening, consider this example. Sarah, Abraham's wife, died when she was 127 years old. The one hundred twenty years denote, in the understanding of numbers, a very long time. To add seven, a perfect number, speaks of an even longer time.[13]

The Hebrew breaks these numbers down even further, as shown on the right side. This is to help define the numbers even more, to the point where Lamech gets sevens in all the columns, making this even more obvious and important. One must remember this information is being offered to those readers of the day, not to us now. This obviously refers to the Babylonian system, which is what is being compared. The sexagesimal system (base 60) used by the Babylonians now comes into play. All of these numbers are expressed using 60, 5, and 7. One scholar has calculated the odds of these ages to be this manner naturally to be one in a hundred million.[14]

Let us consider what this means. Methuselah had Lamech when he was 187 years old. Do the math (60 + 60 + 60 + 7). We can also use this numbering system via months. Adam was 130 when Seth was born (60 + 60 years) + (60 + 60 months) equals 130 years. This way of counting attracts the attention of the readers of that time, especially with the stress of the 5 and 7 as counted.[15] The author added more to the story. Consider the right side of the table above. Here is how the Hebrew notates the ages: for Lamech, 7 *and* 70 *and* 700 years highlights this to the extreme. We can go on and on but will not.

This numbers game shows another side of all this. As calculated from the above table, 1,657 years passed between the origin of man (Adam) to the end of the flood and the restart of life.[16] This does not seem important until we consider Enoch's lifespan of 365 years. This is the same number as days in a year. Continuing, 600,000 is a sexagesimal number indicating a very,

---

13   Do not get goofy here—of course adding another seven years means a longer time. Here in the numerology parlance, we must read this to mean "No seriously, she lived a really long time."

14   Jim Stump, Biologos, October 5, 2017, "Long Life Spans in Genesis: Literal or Symbolic?" https://biologos.org/articles/long-life-spans-in-genesis-literal-or-symbolic.

15   The number to keep in mind is 60: 60 years, 5 years (60 months), and 7 years. Using this counting method, all the ages listed will align.

16   Use the birth ages for this calculation.

very, very long time. Let's play the game now: 600,000 days make 1,643 years (of 365 days). We know Methuselah's age to have a duo of 7 years added (perhaps a clue here). If we add those 14 years to that 1,643, we arrive at 1,657! Very similar to the numbering used by the Babylonians in their Sumerian King List.

But wait, there's more! If we take the number of years until the death of these men, the total is 8,226. Taking half the 600,000 (which is an ordinal number in the sexagesimal system) but instead making them days and dividing by 365 days, we come to 8,219 years. Add 7 years (of course), and we arrive at 8,226 years! How small are the odds for both the start dates and end dates to equal this numbering naturally? Our author definitely planned this, for here is the Torah's goal. The Torah used the SKL as a guide, but to create and refine, quietly and firmly, the idea that men, not gods or semi-divine beings, lived, bore children, and died. We are all one family, with a father and mother who lived with the precept of honoring the god's directive of being fruitful and multiplying.

Taking Out the Trash

For those of you who have perhaps gone down this primrose path before, there is a question I wish to answer now. There are three different dating systems regarding Adam's genealogy. We find the Masoretic, Samaritan, and Septuagint texts, which are regarded as the primary sources when considering the timelines. What is written above is based on the Masoretic textus. It is the basis for our English translations and is in line with the Dead Sea Scrolls. The other two, while very important and concise, have issues—notably with the Septuagint, which is a translation from Hebrew into Greek. What is found inside these works are three differing dating systems, as seen in the table below. At issue here is fiddling with the dates to ensure no one is alive after the flood. Not so nicely put, they needed to kill everyone off prior to the flood because it would not look good for Methuselah to be wandering about when the world was cleansed of everyone but Noah and his crew. The concern was about this purpose, not in keeping the information listed above in pristine order.

	Masoretic			Samaritan			Septuagint		
	1st Son	Til Death	Total	1st Son	Til Death	Total	1st Son	Til Death	Total
Adam	130	800	930	130	800	930	230	700	930
Seth	105	807	912	105	807	912	205	707	912
Enosh	90	815	905	90	815	905	190	715	905
Kenan	70	840	910	70	840	910	170	740	910
Mahalalel	65	830	895	65	830	895	165	730	895
Jared	162	800	962	62	785	847	162	700	862
Enoch	65	300	365	65	300	365	165	200	365
Methuselal	187	782	969	67	653	720	167	802	969
Lamech	182	595	777	53	600	653	188	565	753
Noah	500		500	500		500	500		500
Until Flood	100	350	950	100	350	950	100	350	950

Final Thoughts

Reading old writings is often dull, especially when one does not understand why the work is being produced. Genealogies are dismissed as useless and dumb, yet when placed into context, both socially and theologically, they can yield boundless information, which helps put the reader into a greater appreciation for what is being transmitted. Such is true here. Ten guys who lived a long time ago bore progeny and died are now appreciated in a whole new way. Their story, while cryptic, lends insight and spirit to the whole of the Hebrew story.

This story takes place in the primeval world of Genesis. Are we to take this to mean these men were fantasy, simply to point a theological finger at the Babylonian mythos and laugh at them? Or is there truth in this genealogy? Yes, it is okay to see the accusing finger and also admire the truth at the same time. However, one point in the favor of these people being real is that throughout the ancient world, real people have been given historical relevance by being great men during their time on earth. Whether they were warlords, city rulers, heroes, or landowners of renown, all had their names carried down through the ages. From what scholars can tell, many times the stories are relatable to those people in some way.

Upon reflection, I am unsure if there was a real antagonism from the writer's point of view toward the Babylonian mythos. In this story, the writer is definitely referring to the SKL, but not in the harsh and demeaning way, as is seen in the first Genesis creation story. When knowing the background of how and why Adam's lineage is spoken of, one is able to see the beauty of history as never before.

And that is a good thing to my mind.

Bibliography

Reference Bibles | *These are the Bibles used for reference in this book.*

Alter, Robert, ed., 2018, *The Hebrew Bible: A Translation with Commentary*, first edition, W. W. Norton & Company.

BibleGateway, n.d., https://www.biblegateway.com/. (Used for consultation of the ASV, ESV, KJV, NET, OJB, RSV, YLT versions.)

Hart, David Bentley, ed., 2017, *The New Testament: A Translation*, Yale University Press.

Jewish Publication Society of America, ed., 1980, The Book of Job: *A New Translation According to the Traditional Hebrew Text*, first edition, Jewish Publication Society of America.

Kirby, Peter, 2001–2013, Early Jewish Writings, https://www.earlyjewishwritings.com/.

Pietersma, Albert, and Benjamin G. Wright, eds., 2007, *A New English Translation of the Septuagint: And the Other Greek Translations Traditionally Included under That Title*, Oxford University Press.

Scherman, Nosson, Yaakov Blinder, Avie Gold, and Meir Zlotowitz, eds., 2011, *Tanach: the Jewish scripture: the twenty-four books of the Jewish Bible featuring a contemporary translation with annotated commentary*, first edition, Mesorah Publications.

Scripture 4 All, 2015, "Hebrew Interlinear Bible," https://scripture4all.org/OnlineInterlinear/Hebrew_
Index.htm.

Textus Receptus Bibles, 2022, https://textusreceptusbibles.com/.

Extra-Biblical References | *Included here are regional texts used by neighboring nations. Also included are noncanonical texts referred to in the chapters of this book.*

Academy of Ancient Texts, 2001, "Epic of Gilgamesh," https://www.ancienttexts.org/library/mesopotamian/gilgamesh/.

———, 2001, "The Babylonian Epic of Creation: 'When on High,'" http://www.ancienttexts.org/library/mesopotamian/enuma.html.

Beyerlin, Walter, ed., 1978, *Near Eastern Religious Texts Relating to the Old Testament*, Westminster Press.

Charles, R. H., 2011, *The Book of Jubilees or the Little Genesis*, Watchmaker Publishing.

Charlesworth, James H., 2009, *The Old Testament Pseudepigrapha*. Hendrickson Academic.

Holmes, Michael W., ed., 1999, *The Apostolic Fathers: Greek Texts and English Translations*, Baker Books.

Tigay, Jeffrey H., 2002, *The Evolution of the Gilgamesh Epic*, Bolchazy-Carducci.

Genesis References | *Sources listed here pertain to Genesis strictly, however, they include references to regional texts as well.*

Bailey, Lloyd R., 1989, *Noah: The Person and the Story in History and Tradition*, first edition, University of South Carolina Press.

Blocher, Henri, 1984, *In the Beginning: The Opening Chapters of Genesis*, Inter-Varsity Press.

Cassuto, Umberto, 1978, *A Commentary on the Book of Genesis: Part One: From Adam to Noah*, The Magnus Press.

Coats, George W., 1983, *Genesis with an Introduction to Narrative Literature*, W. B. Eerdmans Publishing Company

———, 1985, 2020, *God's Conflict with the Dragon and the Sea*, Wipf and Stock Publishers.

Craig, William Lane, 2021, *In Quest of the Historical Adam: A Biblical and Scientific Exploration*, W. B. Eerdmans Publishing Company.

Day, John, 2015, *From Creation to Babel: Studies in Genesis 1–11*, T & T Clark.

Finkel, Irving L., 2014, *The Ark before Noah: Decoding the Story of the Flood*, first American edition, Nan A. Talese/Doubleday.

Gunkel, Hermann, and Mark E. Biddle, eds., 1997, *Genesis*, Mercer University Press.

Gunkel, Hermann, and Heinrich Zimmern, 2006, *Creation and Chaos in the Primeval Era and the Eschaton: A Religio-Historical Study of Genesis 1 and Revelation 12*, W. B. Eerdmans Publishing Company.

Johnson, Marshall D., 1969, *The Purpose of the Biblical Genealogies: With Special Reference to the Setting of the Genealogies of Jesus*, Cambridge University Press.

Kass, Leon, 2003, *The Beginning of Wisdom: Reading Genesis*, Free Press.

Kikawada, Isaac M., and Arthur Quinn, 1999, *Before Abraham Was: The Unity of Genesis 1–11*, Wipf & Stock.

Pageau, Matthieu, 2018, *The Language of Creation: Cosmic Symbolism in Genesis: A Commentary*, CreateSpace.

Rad, Gerhard von., 1972, *Genesis: A Commentary*, revised edition, Westminster Press.

———, 1966, *The Problem of the Hexateuch and Other Essays*, McGraw Hill Book Co.

Sarna, Nahum M., 1978, *Understanding Genesis*, Schocken Books.

Wallace, Howard N., 1985, *The Eden Narrative*, Scholars Press.

Westermann, Claus, 1984, *Genesis 1–11: A Commentary*, Augsburg Publishing House.

Zevit, Ziony, 2013, *What Really Happened in the Garden of Eden?*, Yale University Press.

Regional Influences | *Research and discussion of the outside influence of other religions and beliefs are found in these books.*

Neal, Jerry, 2012, *Ugaritic Texts and the Bible*, CreateSpace.

Smith, George, 2018, *The Chaldean Account of Genesis: The Creation, the Fall of Man, the Deluge, the Tower of Babel, the Times of the Patriarchs*, Generation Books.

Van Till, Howard J., ed., 1990, *Portraits of Creation: Biblical and Scientific Perspectives on the World's Formation*, W. B. Eerdmans Publishing Company.

Walton, John H., 2006, *Ancient Near Eastern Thought and the Old Testament: Introducing the Conceptual World of the Hebrew Bible*, Baker Academic.

Wyatt, N., 2001, *Space and Time in the Religious Life of the Near East*, Sheffield Academic Press.

Yamauchi, Edwin M., 1990, *Persia and the Bible*, Baker Book House.

World Realities | *The study of the world around us has led to these works. We must not take these facts as mere misnomers, for these books describe the world as Yahweh created it—past, present, and future.*

Cline, Eric H., 2021, *1177 B.C.: The Year Civilization Collapsed*, revised and updated edition, Princeton University Press.

Dalley, Stephanie, ed., 2008, *Myths from Mesopotamia: Creation, the Flood, Gilgamesh, and Others*, revised edition, Oxford University Press.

Dever, William G., 2020, *Has Archaeology Buried the Bible?*, W. B. Eerdmans Publishing Company.

Finkelstein, Israel, and Neil Asher Silberman, 2006, *David and Solomon: In Search of the Bible's Sacred Kings and the Roots of the Western Tradition*, Free Press.

———, 2001, *The Bible Unearthed: Archaeology's New Vision of Ancient Israel and the Origin of Its Sacred Texts*, Free Press.

Gould, Stephen Jay, 2011, *Rocks of Ages: Science and Religion in the Fullness of Life*, Random House US.

Montgomery, David R., 2012, *The Rocks Don't Lie: A Geologist Investigates Noah's Flood*, first edition, W. W. Norton.

Oden, Robert A., 1987, *The Bible without Theology: The Theological Tradition and Alternatives to It*, first edition, Harper & Row.

Rudwick, M. J. S., 2014, *Earth's Deep History: How It Was Discovered and Why It Matters*, The University of Chicago Press.

Ryan, William B. F. and Walter C. Pitman, 1998, *Noah's Flood: The New Scientific Discoveries about the Event That Changed History*, Simon & Schuster.

Sáenz-Badillos, Angel, 1997, *A History of the Hebrew Language*, Cambridge University Press.

Old Testament References | *Biblical Criticism at its best! Seeing the Old Testament as it is, not as tradition demands.*

Ackroyd, Peter R., 1968, *Exile and Restoration: A Study of Hebrew Thought of the Sixth Century B.C.*, Westminster Press.

Akenson, Donald H., 1998, *Surpassing Wonder: The Invention of the Bible and the Talmuds*, Harcourt Brace.

Albright, William Foxwell, 1957, *From the Stone Age to Christianity*, The John Hopkins Press.

———, 1963, *The Biblical Period from Abraham to Ezra*, Harper & Row.

Alt, Albrecht, trans. R. A. Wilson, 1967, *Essays on Old Testament History and Religion*, Doubleday.

Brueggemann, Walter, and Hans Walter Wolff, 1975, *The Vitality of Old Testament Traditions*, John Knox Press.

Clifford, Richard J., 1972, *The Cosmic Mountain in Canaan and the Old Testament*, Harvard University Press.

———, 2007, *From Eden to Exile: Unraveling Mysteries of the Bible*, National Geographic.

Eissfeldt, Otto, 1966, *The Old Testament: An Introduction*, Basil Blackwell.

Frankfort, Henri, 1977, *The Intellectual Adventure of Ancient Man: An Essay on Speculative Thought in the Ancient Near East*, University of Chicago Press.

Friedman, Richard Elliott, 1995, *The Disappearance of God: A Divine Mystery*, first edition, Little, Brown and Co.

Halpern, Baruch, 1988, *The First Historians: The Hebrew Bible and History*, first edition, Harper & Row.

Kugel, James, 1997, *The Bible as It Was*, Belknap Press of Harvard University Press.

———, 2004, *The God of Old: Inside the Lost World of the Bible*, Free Press.

Kugel, James and Rowan A. Greer, 1986, *Early Biblical Interpretation*, first edition, Westminster Press.

Noth, Martin, 1965, *The History of Israel*, Adam and Charles Black.

Oesterley, W. O. E., and Theodore H. Robinson, 1946, *An Introduction to the Books of the Old Testament*, SPCK.

Rad, Gerhard von, and K. C. Hanson, 2005, *From Genesis to Chronicles: Explorations in Old Testament Theology*, Fortress Press.

Sarna, Nahum M., 1996, *Exploring Exodus: The Origins of Biblical Israel*, Schocken Books.

Soggin, J. Alberto, 1984, *A History of Israel: From the Beginnings to the Bar Kochba Revolt, AD 135*, SCM Press.

———, 1989, *Introduction to the Old Testament: From Its Origins to the Closing of the Alexandrian Canon*, third edition, Westminster/John Knox Press.

Van Seters, John, 1992, *Prologue to History: The Yahwist as Historian in Genesis*, first edition, Westminster/John Knox Press.

Wellhausen, Julius, 1965, *Prolegomena to the History of Ancient Israel*, The World Publishing Co.

Mythic Considerations | *A myth is not a lie. Here are references that help illuminate one's understanding of how people thought and built their histories throughout early times.*

Childs, Brevard S., 1962, *Myth and Reality in the Old Testament*, Wipf & Stock.

Cross, Frank Moore, 1997, *Canaanite Myth and Hebrew Epic: Essays in the History of the Religion of Israel*, Harvard University Press.

Fishbane, Michael A., 2005, *Biblical Myth and Rabbinic Mythmaking*, Oxford University Press.

Frazer, James George, 1988, *Folklore in the Old Testament: Studies in Comparative Religion, Legend, and Law*, Avenel Books: distributed by Crown Publishers.

Graves, Robert, and Raphael Patai, 1983, *Hebrew Myths: The Book of Genesis*, Greenwich House: distributed by Crown Publishers.

Gunkel, Hermann, 1987, *The Folktale in the Old Testament*, Almond Press.

Hughes, Jeremy, 2009, *Secrets of the Times Myth and History in Biblical Chronology*, Bloomsbury T&T Clark.

Kirk, Geoffrey S., 1998, *Myth: Its Meaning and Functions in Ancient and Other Cultures*, University of California Press.

Mac Cormac, Earl R., 1976, *Metaphor and Myth in Science and Religion*, Duke University Press.

McKenzie, John, 1963, *Myths and Realities: Studies in Biblical Theology*. The Bruce Publishing Co.

Various Ideas to Ponder | *Books that consider smaller parts of the Old Testament, although sometimes the authors play a big game. (* Indicates the three books that inspired me to set out on this journey.)*

*Armstrong, Karen, 1994, *A History of God: The 4000-Year Quest of Judaism, Christianity and Islam*, Ballantine Books.

Assmann, Jan, 2001, *The Search for God in Ancient Egypt*, first English-language edition with revisions and additions, Cornell University Press.

Burrows, Millar, 1986, *The Dead Sea Scrolls*, Gramercy Publishing Co.

*Cross, Frank Moore, 2000, *From Epic to Canon: History and Literature in Ancient Israel*, J. Hopkins University Press.

Friedman, Richard Elliott, ed., 2003, *The Bible with Sources Revealed: A New View into the Five Books of Moses*, first edition, HarperSanFrancisco.

———, 1998, *The Hidden Book in the Bible*, first edition, HarperSanFrancisco.

Rosenberg, David, and Harold Bloom, eds., 1990, The Book of J, first edition, Grove Weidenfeld.

Smith, Mark S., 2002, *The Early History of God: Yahweh and the Other Deities in Ancient Israel*, second edition, W. B. Eerdmans Publishing Company.

Smith, Morton, 1987, *Palestinian Parties and Politics That Shaped the Old Testament*, SCM Press.

Swanson, Guy E., 1960, *The Birth of the Gods: The Origin of Primitive Beliefs*, University of Michigan Press.

*Wright, Robert, 2010, *The Evolution of God*, Back Bay Books.

The Church Today | *Freeing oneself from the demands of tradition allows one to see the beauty of the Bible. These books consider the impact of biblical criticism against the constraints of evangelical fundamentalism.*

Barr, James, 1984, *Beyond Fundamentalism*, first American edition, Westminster Press.

———, 1978, *Fundamentalism*, Westminster Press.

Borg, Marcus J., 2001, *Reading the Bible Again for the First Time: Taking the Bible Seriously but Not Literally*, first edition, HarperSanFrancisco.

Childs, Brevard S., 1970, *Biblical Theology in Crisis*, Westminster Press.

Harrisville, Roy A., and Walter Sundberg, 1995, *The Bible in Modern Culture: Theology and Historical-Critical Method from Spinoza to Käsemann*, W. B. Eerdmans Publishing Company.

Hays, Christopher M., ed., 2013, *Evangelical Faith and the Challenge of Historical Criticism*, Baker Academic.

McKenzie, Steven L., and Stephen R. Haynes, eds., 1999, *To Each Its Own Meaning: An Introduction to Biblical Criticisms and Their Application*, revised and expanded, John Knox Press.

Noll, Mark A., 1986, *Between Faith and Criticism: Evangelicals, Scholarship, and the Bible in America*, first edition, Harper & Row.

Pratchett, Terry, 1992, *Small Gods: A Novel of Discworld*, first U.S. edition, HarperCollins.

Smith, Christian, 2011, *The Bible Made Impossible: Why Biblicism Is Not a Truly Evangelical Reading of Scripture*, Brazos.

Spinoza, Benedictus de, R. H. M. Elwes, and Benedictus de Spinoza, 2004, *A Theologico-Political Treatise* and *A Political Treatise*, Dover Publications.

Tov, Emanuel, 1992, *Textual Criticism of the Hebrew Bible*, Fortress Press.

Wegner, Paul D., 2006, *A Student's Guide to Textual Criticism of the Bible: Its History, Methods & Results*, IVP Academic/InterVarsity Press.

Yovel, Yirmiyahu, 1989, *Spinoza and Other Heretics*, Princeton University Press.

www.ingramcontent.com/pod-product-compliance
Lightning Source LLC
Chambersburg PA
CBHW051144120626
46547CB00012B/941